Workshop on Intelligent Interactive Systems and Language Generation (2IS&NLG 2018)

Tilburg, The Netherlands
5 November 2018

ISBN: 978-1-5108-7756-6

Printed from e-media with permission by:

Curran Associates, Inc.
57 Morehouse Lane
Red Hook, NY 12571

Some format issues inherent in the e-media version may also appear in this print version.

Printed by Curran Associates, Inc. (2019)

For permission requests, please contact the Association for Computational Linguistics at the address below.

Association for Computational Linguistics
209 N. Eighth Street
Stroudsburg, Pennsylvania 18360

Phone: 1-570-476-8006
Fax: 1-570-476-0860

acl@aclweb.org

Additional copies of this publication are available from:

Curran Associates, Inc.
57 Morehouse Lane
Red Hook, NY 12571 USA
Phone: 845-758-0400
Fax: 845-758-2633
Email: curran@proceedings.com
Web: www.proceedings.com

2IS&NLG 2018

Workshop on
Intelligent Interactive Systems and Language Generation

Proceedings of the Workshop

November 5, 2018
Tilburg, The Netherlands

Order copies of this and other ACL proceedings from:

Association for Computational Linguistics (ACL)
209 N. Eighth Street
Stroudsburg, PA 18360
USA
Tel: +1-570-476-8006
Fax: +1-570-476-0860
acl@aclweb.org

Introduction

Welcome to the Proceedings of the Workshop on Intelligent Interactive Systems and Language Generation (2IS&NLG 2018)! This workshop seeks to gather researchers and practitioners working on language generation, human-computer interaction, conversational agents, and computational intelligence that deal with cross-cutting issues concerning language generation and intelligent interactive systems. It is to be held on November 5 2018 at the International Conference on Natural Language Generation (INLG2018), which is supported by the Special Interest Group on NLG of the Association for Computational Linguistics.

We received 16 submissions (13 regular papers and 3 demos). 9 regular submissions were accepted after a double blind peer review, whereas 2 demos have been included in the program after a juried process. In addition, 2IS&NLG 2018 included an invited talk by Sander Wubben (Tilburg University).

We would like to thank to all authors for submitting their contributions to our workshop. We thank the program committee members for their work at reviewing the papers and their support during the organization.

Jose M. Alonso, Alejandro Catala and Mariët Theune
2IS&NLG 2018 Organizers

Workshop Organizers:

Jose M. Alonso, University of Santiago de Compostela
Alejandro Catala, University of Santiago de Compostela
Mariët Theune, University of Twente

Program Committee:

Alejandro Catala, CiTIUS, University of Santiago de Compostela
Jose M. Alonso, University of Santiago de Compostela
Lorenzo Gatti, HMI lab, University of Twente
Anna Wilbik, Eindhoven University of Technology
Simon Mille, Universitat Pompeu Fabra
Mariët Theune, University of Twente
Daniel Sanchez, University of Granada
Amy Isard, The University of Edinburgh
Andreea I. Niculescu, A*STAR
Ondrej Dusek, Heriot-Watt University
Pablo Gervás, Universidad Complutense de Madrid
Martín Pereira-Fariña University of Santiago de Compostela
Marcos Garcia, University of A Coruna
Alejandro Ramos, University of Santiago de Compostela
Alberto Bugarín, University of Santiago de Compostela
Ehud Reiter University of Aberdeen
Dirk Heylen University of Twente
Nicolas Szilas, TECFA-FPSE, University of Geneva
Georgios N. Yannakakis, University of Malta

Invited Speaker:

Sander Wubben, Tilburg University

Table of Contents

Workshop Program

Monday, November 5, 2018

9:00–9:15	**Introduction**
9:15–10:15	**Invited Talk by Dr. Sander Wubben on "Applications of NLG in practical conversational AI settings"**
10:15–10:45	**Spotlight pitches**
10:45–11:30	**Coffee/Tea Break**
11:30–11:55	**Interactive Poster & Demo session – Round 1**
11:55–12:20	**Interactive Poster & Demo session – Round 2**
12:20–12:30	**Wrap up**

Invited talk

Applications of NLG in practical conversational AI settings

Sander Wubben
s.wubben@tilburguniversity.edu

Tilburg center for Cognition and Communication (TiCC)
Tilburg University, The Netherlands

Abstract

Conversational AI has seen a surge in popularity recently with the rise of chatbots and smart speakers such as Amazon Alexa and Google Home. A logical extension of this development that can be expected is a rise in popularity of NLG in such settings, as the task of such a conversational system consists mainly of producing an output in natural language for a given language input. However, the extent to which NLG has seen adoption in conversational settings has been limited so far. In this talk I will give an overview to which extent NLG is used for conversational AI in the Flow.ai conversational AI platform. I will discuss training an end-to-end recurrent neural network on various data sets to build conversational systems, give an overview of the evaluation and discuss what can be expected of such systems in a practical setting. I will also discuss other uses of NLG within conversational AI, ranging from basic slot filling to more advanced functionality such as generation of data for the training of conversational AI agents or to support humans in customer service settings by providing template responses in order to decrease response times.

Proceedings of the Workshop on Intelligent Interactive Systems and Language Generation (2IS&NLG), pages 1–2,
Tilburg, The Netherlands, November 5 2018.

Generating Descriptions for Sequential Images with Local-Object Attention and Global Semantic Context Modelling

Jing Su[1], Chenghua Lin[2], Mian Zhou[3], Qingyun Dai[4], Haoyu Lv[4]
[1]Guangdong Ocean University, [2]University of Aberdeen
[3] Tianjin University of Technology, [4] Guangdong University of Technology
jingsuw@163.com, chenghua.lin@abdn.ac.uk
zhoumian@tjut.edu.cn, 1144295091@qq.com, lvhaoyuchn@163.com

Abstract

In this paper, we propose an end-to-end CNN-LSTM model for generating descriptions for sequential images with a local-object attention mechanism. To generate coherent descriptions, we capture global semantic context using a multi-layer perceptron, which learns the dependencies between sequential images. A paralleled LSTM network is exploited for decoding the sequence descriptions. Experimental results show that our model outperforms the baseline across three different evaluation metrics on the datasets published by Microsoft.

1 Introduction

Recently, automatically generating image descriptions has attracted considerable interest in the fields of computer vision and nature language processing. Such a task is easy to humans but highly non-trivial for machines as it requires not only capturing the semantic information from images (e.g., objects and actions) but also needs to generate human-like natural language descriptions.

Existing approaches to generating image description are dominated by neural network-based methods, which mostly focus on generating description for a single image (Karpathy and Li, 2015; Xu et al., 2015; Jia et al., 2015; You et al., 2016). Generating descriptions for sequential images, in contrast, is much more challenging, i.e., the information of both individual images as well as the dependencies between images in a sequence needs to be captured.

Huang et al. (2016) introduce the first sequential vision-to-language dataset and exploit Gated Recurrent Units (GRUs) (Cho et al., 2014) based encoder and decoder for the task of visual storytelling. However, their approach only considers image information of a sequence at the first time step of the decoder, where the local attention mechanism is ignored which is important for capturing the correlation between the features of an individual image and the corresponding words in a description sentence. Yu et al. (2017) propose a hierarchically-attentive Recurrent Neural Nets (RNNs) for album summarisation and storytelling. To generate descriptions for an image album, their hierarchical framework selects representative images from several image sequences of the album, where the selected images might not necessary have correlation to each other.

In this paper, we propose an end-to-end CNN-LSTM model with a local-object attention mechanism for generating story-like descriptions for multiple images of a sequence. To improve the coherence of the generated descriptions, we exploit a paralleled long short-terms memory (LSTM) network and learns global semantic context by embedding the global features of sequential images as an initial input to the hidden layer of the LSTM model. We evaluate the performance of our model on the task of generating story-like descriptions for an image sequence on the sequence-in-sequence (SIS) dataset published by Microsoft. We hypothesise that by taking into account global context, our model can also generate better descriptions for individual images. Therefore, in another set of experiments, we further test our model on the Descriptions of Images-in-Isolation (DII) dataset for generating descriptions for each individual image of a sequence. Experimental results show that our model outperforms a baseline developed based on the state-of-the-art image captioning model (Xu et al., 2015) in terms of BLEU, METEOR and ROUGE, and can generate sequential descriptions which preserve the dependencies between sentences.

Proceedings of the Workshop on Intelligent Interactive Systems and Language Generation (2IS&NLG), pages 3–8,
Tilburg, The Netherlands, November 5 2018.

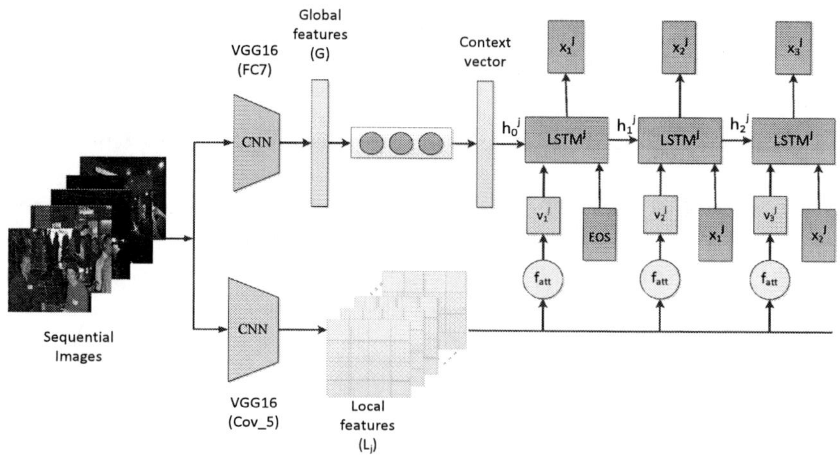

Figure 1: The architecture of our CNN-LSTM model with global semantic context.

2 Related Work

Recent successes in machine translation using Recurrent Neural Network (RNN) (Bahdanau et al., 2014; Cho et al., 2014) catalyse the adoption of neural networks in the task of image caption generation. Early works of image caption generation based on CNN-RNN networks have been made great progress.Vinyals et al. (2014) propose an encoder-decoder model which utilises a Convolutional Neural Network (CNN) for encoding the input image into a vector representation and a Recurrent Neural Network (RNN) for decoding the corresponding text description. Similarly, Karpathy and Li (2015) present an alignment model based on a CNN and a bidirectional RNN which can align segment regions of an image to the corresponding words of a text description. Donahue et al. (2014) propose a Long-term Recurrent Convolutional Network (LRCN) which integrates convolutional layers and long-range temporal recursion for generating image descriptions.

Recently, the attention mechanism (Xu et al., 2015; You et al., 2016; Lu et al., 2016; Zhou et al., 2016) has been widely used and proved to be effective in the task of image description generation. For instance, Xu et al. (2015) explore two kinds of attention mechanism for generating image descriptions, i.e., soft-attention and hard-attention, whereas You et al. (2016) exploits a selective semantic attention mechanism for the same task.

There is also a surge of research interest in visual storytelling (Kim and Xing, 2014; Sigurdsson et al., 2016; Huang et al., 2016; Yu et al., 2017). Huang et al. (2016) collect stories using Mechanical Turk and translate a sequence of images into story-like descriptions by extending a GRU-GRU framework. Yu et al. (2017) utilise a hierarchically-attentive structures with combined RNNs for photo selection and story generation. However, the above mentioned approaches for generating descriptions of sequential images do not explicitly capture the dependencies between each individual images of a sequence, which is the gap that we try to address in this paper.

3 Methodology

In this section, we describe the proposed CNN-LSTM model with local-object attention. In order to generate coherent descriptions for an image sequence, we introduce global semantic context and a paralleled LSTM in our framework as shown in Figure. 1. Our model works by first extracting the global features of sequential images using a CNN network (VGG16) (Simonyan and Zisserman, 2014), which has been extensively used in image recognition. Here a VGG16 model contains 13 convolutional layers, 5 pooling layers and 3 fully connected layers. The extracted global features are then embedded into a global semantic vector with a multi-layer perceptron as the initial input to the hidden layer of a paralleled LSTM model. Our model then applies the last convolutional-layer operation from the VGG16 model to generate the local features of each image in sequence. Finally, we introduce a paralleled LSTM model and a local-object attention mechanism to decode sentence descriptions.

3.1 Features Extraction and Embedding

Sequential image descriptions are different from single image description due to the spatial correlation between images. Therefore, in the encoder, we exploit both global and local features for describing the content of sequential images. We extract global features of the sequential images with the second fully connected layer (FC7) from VGG16 model. The global features are denoted by G which are a set of 4096-dimension vectors. Then, we select the features of the final convolutional layer (Cov_5) from the VGG16 model to represent local features for each image in the sequence. The local features are denoted as L_j ($j = 1,...,N$), where N is the number of images in the sequence. In our experiment, we follow Huang et al. (2016) and set 5 as the number of images in a sequence. Finally, we embed the global features G into a 512-dimension context vector via a multilayer perceptron which is then used as the initial input of the hidden layer in LSTM model.

3.2 Sequential Descriptions Generation

In the decoding stage, our goal is to obtain the most likely text descriptions of a given sequence of images. This can be generated by training a model to maximize the log likelihood of a sequence of sentences S, given the corresponding sequential images I and the model parameters θ, as shown in Eq. 1.

$$\theta^* = \arg\max_{\theta} \sum_{j=1}^{N} \sum_{(I,s_j)} log\, p(s_j|I,\theta) \quad (1)$$

Here s_j denotes a sentence in S, and N is the total number of sentences in S.

Assuming a generative model of each sentence s_j produces each word in the sentence in order, the log probability of s_j is given by the sum of the log probabilities over the words:

$$\log p(s_j|I) = \sum_{t=1}^{C} log\, p(s_{j,t}|I, s_{j,1}, s_{j,2}...s_{j,t-1}) \quad (2)$$

where $s_{j,t}$ represents the tth word in the jth sentence and C is the total number of words of s_j.

We utilize a LSTM network (Hochreiter and Schmidhuber, 1997) to produce a sequence descriptions conditioned on the local feature vectors, the previous generated words, as well as the hidden state with a global semantic context. Formally, our LSTM model is formulated as follows:

$$\begin{aligned} i_t^j &= \sigma(W_{xi}x_{t-1}^j + W_{hi}h_{t-1}^j + W_{vi}v_t^j + b_i) \\ f_t^j &= \sigma(W_{xf}x_{t-1}^j + W_{hf}h_{t-1}^j + W_{vf}v_t^j + b_f) \\ o_t^j &= \sigma(W_{xo}x_{t-1}^j + W_{ho}h_{t-1}^j + W_{vo}v_t^j + b_o) \\ q_t^j &= \varphi(W_{xq}x_{t-1}^j + W_{hq}h_{t-1}^j + W_{vq}v_t^j + b_q) \\ c_t^j &= f_t^j \odot c_{t-1}^j + i_t^j \odot q_t^j \\ h_t^j &= o_t^j \odot \varphi(c_t^j) \end{aligned} \quad (3)$$

where i_t^j, f_t^j, o_t^j and c_t^j represents input gates, forget gates, output gates and memory, respectively. q_t^j represents the updating information in the memory c_t^j. σ denotes the sigmoid activation function, $\odot$ represents the element-wise multiplication, and φ indicates the hyperbolic tangent function. $W_\bullet$ and $b_\bullet$ are the parameters to be estimated during training. Also h_t^j is the hidden state at time step t which will be used as an input to the LSTM unit at the next time step.

Here, we utilize a multilayer perceptron to model the global semantic context which can be viewed as the initial input of the hidden state h_0^j, where every initial value h_0^j in the LSTM model is equal and is defined as:

$$h_0^j = W_0\, \varphi(W_g G + b_g) \quad (4)$$

When modelling local context, the local context vector v_t^j is a dynamic representation of the relevant part of the jth image in a sequence at time t. In Eq. 6, we use the attention mechanism f_{att} proposed by (Bahdanau et al., 2014) to compute the local attention vector v_t^j, where the corresponding weight k_t^j of each local features L_j is computed by a softmax function with input from a multilayer perceptron which considers both the current local vector L_j and the hidden state h_{t-1}^j at time $t-1$.

$$k_t^j = softmax(W_k\, tanh(W_{lv}L^j + W_{hv}h_{t-1}^j + b_v)) \quad (5)$$

$$v_t^j = \sum_{i=1}^{M} k_{it}^j L_i^j \quad (6)$$

4 Experiments

Dataset.

Both the SIS and DII datasets are published by Microsoft[1], which have a similar data structure,

[1] http://visionandlanguage.net/VIST/

DII (our model)	(1) a group of people that are on the beach. (2) a man and a woman pose for a picture together. (3) a city at night with many buildings in the backgroud. (4) a bridge that is next to the water. (5) a large ship is being enjoyed by the crowd.
DII (cnn-att-lstm)	(1) a group of people that are next to each other. (2) a man and a woman sitting at a table. (3) a group of friends pose for a picture. (4) the man is blowing out into the camera. (5) a woman is smilling.
DII (ground truth)	(1) a variety of people sitting in a window filled restanrant. (2) closeup of a woman looking to her right in a restaurant setting. (3) many buildings by the beach. (4) a waterfront scence from an outside restaurant at night. (5) people on the ferris wheel.
SIS (our model)	(1) the family went to restaurant. (2) the family was very excited to have a party. (3) the sun was going down to the beach. (4) the family decide to go to restaurant. (5) i was so excited to have a great time.
SIS (cnn-att-lstm)	(1) the city is a small windows. (2) the girls are ready to go to the day. (3) the beautiful fireworks. (4) the city has a great view. (5) we drove up.
SIS (ground truth)	(1) me and my lover went on a vacation to see some sights. here we are getting something to eat. (2) we liked the food but the place was rather crowded for our tastes. here is a view of the city from our hotel. (3) it was so lovely to look out every night as the sun went down. another shot from high up. (4) it was breath taking to watch the city light up as the sun went down. (5) we where in line for a ferris wheel. i thought that this would make a good pic, and i think it came out well.

Figure 2: Example of sequential descriptions generated by our model, the baseline, and the ground truth.

Positive example

(1) the kids had a lot of fun. (2) the people were very happy to celebrate. (3) the people brought their favorite. (4) the people were enjoying themselves. (5) the people were very happy.

Failure Example

(1) there was a great time. (2) i had a great time. (3) we took a great time. (4) this is a picture. (5) we had a great time.

Figure 3: Error analysis of our model. First row: our model generates correct captions. Second row: failure cases due to severe overfitting.

Dataset	Train	Test	Vocab. Size
DII	23,415	1,665	10,000
SIS	110,905	10,370	18,000

Table 1: Dataset statistics.

Dataset	Method	BLEU	METEOR	ROUGE
DII	cnn-att-lstm	36.1	9.2	26.9
	Our model	**40.1**	**11.2**	**29.1**
SIS	cnn-att-lstm	15.2	4.6	13.6
	Our model	**17.2**	**5.5**	**15.2**

Table 2: Evaluation of the quality of descriptions generated for sequential images.

i.e., each image sequence consists of five images and their corresponding descriptions. The key difference is that descriptions of SIS consider the dependencies between images, whereas the descriptions of DII are generated for each individual image, i.e., no dependencies are considered. As the full DII and SIS datasets are quite large, we only used part of both datasets for our initial experiments, where the dataset statistics are shown in Table 1.

Evaluation. We compare our model with the sequence-to-sequence baseline (cnn-att-lstm) with attention mechanism (Xu et al., 2015). The cnn-att-lstm baseline only utilises the local attention mechanism which combines visual concepts of an image with the corresponding words in a sentence. Our model, apart from adopting a local-object attention, can further model global semantic context for capturing the correlation between sequential images.

Table 2 shows the experimental results of our model on the task of generating descriptions for sequential images with three popular evaluation metrics, i.e. BLEU, Meteor and ROUGE. It can be observed from Table 2 that our model outperforms the baseline on both SIS and DII datasets for all evaluation metrics. It is also observed that the scores of the evaluation metric are generally higher for the DII dataset than the SIS dataset. The main reason is that the SIS dataset contains more sentences descriptions in a sequence and more abstract content descriptions such as "breathtaking" and "excited" which are difficult to understand and prone to overfitting.

Figure 2 shows an example sequence of five images as well as their corresponding descriptions generated by our model, the baseline (cnn-att-lstm), and the ground truth. For the SIS dataset, it can observed that our model can capture more coherent story-like descriptions. For instance, our model can learn the social word "family" to connect the whole story and learn the emotional words "great time" to summarise the description. However, the baseline model failed to capture such important information. Our model can learn dependencies of visual scenes between images even on the DII dataset. For example, compared to the descriptions generated by cnn-att-lstm, our model can learn the visual word "beach" in image 1 by reasoning from the visual word "water" in image 4.

Our model can generally achieve good results by capturing the global semantics of an image sequence such as the example in the first row of Figure 3. However, our model also has difficulties in generating meaningful descriptions in a number of cases. For instance, our model generates fairly abstractive descriptions such as "a great time" due to severe overfitting, as shown in the second row of Figure 3. We suppose the issue of overfitting is likely to be alleviated by adding more training data or using more effective algorithm for image feature extraction.

5 Conclusion

In this paper, we present a local-object attention model with global semantic context for sequential image descriptions. Unlike other CNN-LSTM models that only employ a single image as input for image caption, our proposed method can generate descriptions of sequential images by exploiting the global semantic context to learn the dependencies between sequential images. Extensive experiments on two image datasets (DII and SIS) show promising results of our model.

Acknowledgement

We thank Ehud Reiter and Kees van Deemter for their helpful discussion. This paper was also supported partly by Science and Technology Project of Guangdong Province (No.503314759024).

References

Dzmitry Bahdanau, Kyunghyun Cho, and Yoshua Bengio. 2014. Neural machine translation by jointly learning to align and translate. *Computer Science*.

Kyunghyun Cho, Bart Van Merrienboer, Caglar Gulcehre, Dzmitry Bahdanau, Fethi Bougares, Holger

Schwenk, and Yoshua Bengio. 2014. Learning phrase representations using rnn encoder-decoder for statistical machine translation. *Computer Science*.

Jeff Donahue, Lisa Anne Hendricks, Sergio Guadarrama, Marcus Rohrbach, Subhashini Venugopalan, Kate Saenko, and Trevor Darrell. 2014. Long-term recurrent convolutional networks for visual recognition and description. *CoRR*.

Sepp Hochreiter and Jürgen Schmidhuber. 1997. Long short-term memory. *Neural Computation*, 9(8):1735–1780.

Ting-Hao (Kenneth) Huang, Francis Ferraro, Nasrin Mostafazadeh, Ishan Misra, Aishwarya Agrawal, Jacob Devlin, Ross Girshick, Xiaodong He, Pushmeet Kohli, Dhruv Batra, C. Lawrence Zitnick, Devi Zitnick Zitnick, Lucy Vanderwende, Michel Galley, and Margaret Mitchell. 2016. Visual storytelling. In *the Conference of the North American Chapter of the Association for Computational Linguistics*, pages 1233–1239.

Xu Jia, Efstratios Gavves, Basura Fernando, and Tinne Tuytelaars. 2015. Guiding the long-short term memory model for image caption generation. In *IEEE International Conference on Computer Vision*, pages 2407–2415.

Andrej Karpathy and Fei Fei Li. 2015. Deep visual-semantic alignments for generating image descriptions. In *Computer Vision and Pattern Recognition*, pages 3128–3137.

G. Kim and E. P. Xing. 2014. Reconstructing storyline graphs for image recommendation from web community photos. In *2014 IEEE Conference on Computer Vision and Pattern Recognition*, pages 3882–3889.

Jiasen Lu, Caiming Xiong, Devi Parikh, and Richard Socher. 2016. Knowing when to look: Adaptive attention via A visual sentinel for image captioning. *CoRR*.

Gunnar A. Sigurdsson, Xinlei Chen, and Abhinav Gupta. 2016. Learning visual storylines with skipping recurrent neural networks. *CoRR*, abs/1604.04279.

Karen Simonyan and Andrew Zisserman. 2014. Very deep convolutional networks for large-scale image recognition. *Computer Science*.

Oriol Vinyals, Alexander Toshev, Samy Bengio, and Dumitru Erhan. 2014. Show and tell: A neural image caption generator. pages 3156–3164.

Kelvin Xu, Jimmy Ba, Ryan Kiros, Kyunghyun Cho, Aaron Courville, Ruslan Salakhutdinov, Richard Zemel, and Yoshua Bengio. 2015. Show, attend and tell: Neural image caption generation with visual attention. *Computer Science*, pages 2048–2057.

Quanzeng You, Hailin Jin, Zhaowen Wang, Chen Fang, and Jiebo Luo. 2016. Image captioning with semantic attention. pages 4651–4659.

Licheng Yu, Mohit Bansal, and Tamara L. Berg. 2017. Hierarchically-attentive RNN for album summarization and storytelling. *CoRR*.

Luowei Zhou, Chenliang Xu, Parker A. Koch, and Jason J. Corso. 2016. Image caption generation with text-conditional semantic attention. *CoRR*.

Automation and Optimisation of Humor Trait Generation in a Vocal Dialogue System

Matthieu Riou
CERI-LIA, Université d'Avignon
matthieu.riou@alumni.univ-avignon.fr

Stéphane Huet
CERI-LIA, Université d'Avignon
stephane.huet@univ-avignon.fr

Bassam Jabaian
CERI-LIA, Université d'Avignon
bassam.jabaian@univ-avignon.fr

Fabrice Lefèvre
CERI-LIA, Université d'Avignon
fabrice.lefevre@univ-avignon.fr

Abstract

This study pertains to our ongoing work about social artificial vocal interactive agents and their adaptation to users. In this regard, several possibilities to introduce humorous productions in a spoken dialogue system are investigated in order to enhance naturalness during interactions between the agent and the user. Our goal is twofold: automation and optimisation of the humor trait generation process. In this regard, a reinforcement learning scheme is proposed allowing to optimise the usage of humor modules in accordance with user preferences. Some simulated experiments are carried out to confirm that the trained policy used by the humor manager is able to converge to a predefined user profile. Then, some user trials are done to evaluate both the nature of the produced humor and its timely and proportionate usage.

1 Introduction

Interactive artificial agents, like spoken dialogue systems, can now support a broad range of applications such as technical support services or reservation systems (for flights, accommodation, restaurant, etc.). For a while, systems used patterns and rules to define their behaviours, e.g. (Rambow et al., 2001). Lately, stochastic-based models have replaced and improved this rule-based approach for all the components of dialogue systems (Young et al., 2013). These more advanced systems offer new possibilities, like a higher variability in their answers or higher flexibility to adapt to specific user preferences. Their downside is that they require a large amount of data to be trained.

In our ongoing work, we are interested in generating traits of humor in the outputs of a spoken dialogue system, to improve user experience and involvement. This paper investigates the opportunities offered by stochastic approaches to train artificial agents to produce humorous answers according to predetermined levels defining their nature and quantity.

Since humor has played an important role in cultural and social life of human beings, similar beneficial consequences can be expected in human-computer interfaces to improve their social competence (Niculescu et al., 2013). Several works attempted to document some theories or explanations on how humor works in general (Mulder and Nijholt, 2002; Bucaria, 2004; Goldwasser and Zhang, 2016) or even questioned the bare possibility to implement it in computers (Ritchie, 2009). Several studies have also been led to define computational rules for generating puns and riddles (Binsted and Ritchie, 1997; Ritchie, 2005; Hempelmann et al., 2006; Anthony Hong and Ong, 2009). Many of the solutions proposed in these papers have inspired our own modules described in the next section. However, while they only studied one phenomenon at a time, the approach presented here combines the existing possible computational ways to produce several humorous traits.

In this work, we are also interested in optimising this new capacity using reinforcement learning. As users can enjoy or reject agent's humor in general, and appreciate a specific type of humor, we want to allow the system to adapt its use of humor mechanisms, both in quantity and quality. We plan to follow an approach similar to the one used at the dialogue management level (Daubigney et al., 2012), so as to let the system choose, at each step, in an informed way, whether or not it is profitable to produce a humor-

Proceedings of the Workshop on Intelligent Interactive Systems and Language Generation (2IS&NLG), pages 9–14,
Tilburg, The Netherlands, November 5 2018.

ous utterance.

This study is, to the best of our knowledge, among the very first to both compile several means to produce humor in an automatic manner along with a process to train such capacity so as to adapt it to user preferences in the matter. It is worth mentioning also that humor is not considered in our work with the only objective to make laugh but more generally to ease the on-going interaction.

In this paper, Section 2 describes different options we investigated to introduce humor in an artificial agent. In Section 3 a framework to optimise the usage of humor in a goal-directed dialogue system is introduced. Then Section 4 presents the experimental work to evaluate this newly trained humorous system and we conclude in Section 5.

2 Humor Generation Modules

As our main objective here is to be able to optimise the usage of humor traits during dialogues, in this preliminary setup, only four humor generation modules are explored (Desfrançois, 2016). The natural language generation module is in charge of combining the humor modules' output with the next dialogue act selected by the dialogue manager in the smoothest way (several modalities are introduced as pre and post humor glues to standard system's outputs).

The **quote** module finds a humorous citation in relation to the user input, so as to remain close to the context of the dialogue. A corpus of purposeful citations collected on-line has been indexed and a query is built from the keywords available in the user's sentence. Quote results of the information retrieval system are ranked for each query according to their distance to a context vector. This distance is used as an indicator of the interest of using the quote in the situation. A threshold has been manually defined to discard cases where no quote is close enough to the user's input. A history is kept to avoid repeating the same quotes.

The **joke** module has a modus operandi similar to the quote module; it returns the jokes that are closest to the context and keeps a history to avoid repetitions. The indexed jokes are generally longer than the quotes and can be used alone, which presupposes a new user turn before returning to the main flow of the dialogue.

Self-derision is also considered, seen as a humorous signal of low-esteem intended to encourage further use of the system by admitting its errors. The module outputs predefined humorous sentences like "Luckily I am not a human", "I will eventually file a complaint against the guy who programed the system" when the dialogue manager can assess that it is in a poor situation.

3 Reinforcement Learning Paradigm for Humor Management

The introduction of the new modules described in the previous section makes a real difference in the system behaviour but their effects are complex to evaluate. The use of Reinforcement Learning (RL) techniques for the optimisation of this new capacity can be a good solution. Since each user can appreciate or reject the humor of the conversational agent, the system will be able to adapt its use of humorous mechanisms.

The dialogue manager used in this paper adapts a system presented in (Ferreira and Lefèvre, 2015). It is based on a dialogue management framework based on a Partially Observable Markov Decision Process (POMDP), the Hidden Information State (HIS) (Young et al., 2010). In this setup, the system maintains a distribution over possible dialogue states (the belief state) and uses it to generate an adequate answer. An RL algorithm, the KTDQ learning algorithm (Geist and Pietquin, 2010), is used to train the system by maximizing an expected cumulative discounted reward, according to two types of feedbacks.

The global feedback is given at the end of the dialogue by asking the user if the entire dialogue is a success or not. The social feedback is given at each turn to score the last response only. It is composed of two parts, the score given by the user to this last response, and the turn cost which penalises too long dialogues by adding a negative score for each turn taken. At the end of the dialogue, the policy is updated according to all the collected feedbacks.

In order to decide when to include a given humor trait with the four generation modules, a policy specific to humor is defined. For this purpose, a dialogue server is launched and consults at each turn of the dialogue system a humor manager. This manager is associated with a policy that is learned with simulated users (see Section 3.2). The following section describes the state space of the humor policy.

3.1 Humor State

The state space for humor is defined by five continuous parameters, each associated with Radial Basis Functions (RBF) to parameterize the policy (Daubigney et al., 2012): percentage of the system utterances with a quotation, a joke, a slip of the tongue, a self-derision assertion or without any trait of humor. All these parameters are defined in the $[0; 1]$ range and converted with RBF into 3 values, which results in a 15-dimension state.

The action space itself contains five different actions: four associated with the humor modules and one for avoiding humor. The number of actions could be extended in order to include a new type of humor module, and the framework has means to capitalise on the simpler policy and avoid starting the learning process from scratch again.

Rewards are defined by a simulated user during simulations from a linear interpolation of the dialogue final score $scoreFinalDialogue$ with respect to the goal, and the humor score $scoreHumor$ from the user's point of view:

$$\begin{aligned} r_f &= \text{wDialogue} \times \text{scoreFinalDialogue} \\ &\quad + \text{wHumor} \times \text{scoreHumor} \ . \end{aligned}$$

$wDialogue$ and $wHumor$ represent the weights of dialogue and humor scores respectively.

The humor score is derived from the satisfaction score computed from the simulated user:

$$\text{scoreHumor} = \text{satisfaction} \times \text{MaxReward} \ .$$

Depending on the percentage of humor matches made during the dialogue and its profile, satisfaction is calculated thanks to the number of humorous actions coherent with the user's preferences. MaxReward is the maximum reward that can be obtained during a dialogue, and so scoreHumor is the reward obtained in a particular dialogue.

3.2 Humor Simulator

For this study an agenda-based user simulator has been extended to take into account humor traits generated by the system. At this point it was not possible to simulate a real appreciation of the quality and pertinence of the generated humor. Hence, only the type and quantity of humor were taken into account. For that purpose, a user's profile was defined, supposed to represent acceptable quantity of each type of possible humor of a specific user. Then, the user simulator was able to reward the simulated dialogues by weighting their success in accordance with its defined profile. From all the possible profiles a few mean profiles were defined as gold standards with a moderate but diversified level of humor, and used for the field trials.

4 Experimental Study

4.1 Task Description

Experiments presented in this paper concern a chit-chat dialogue system framed in a goal-oriented dialogue task. In this context, users discuss with the system about an image (out of a small predefined set of 6), and they tried jointly to discover the message conveyed by the image, as described in (Chaminade, 2017). In order to use a goal-oriented system for such a task, the principle which has been followed was to construct, as the system's back-end, a database containing several hundreds of possible combinations of characteristics of the image, each associated with a hypothesis of the conveyed message. During its interaction with the system, it is expected that the user progressively gives elements from the image, which matches entities in the database. In return, the system selects a small subset of possible entities to inform the user or ultimately provides a pre-defined message to give as a plausible explanation for the image's purpose. Thus, the user can speak rather freely about the image before arguing briefly about the message. No argumentation is possible from the system's side, it can only propose a canned message and the discussion is expected to last only around one minute at most.

The task-dependent knowledge base used in the experiments is derived from INT task description (Chaminade, 2017), as well as from a generic dialogue information. The semantics of the task is represented by 16 different act types, 9 slots and 51 values. The lexical forms (53) used to model act types were manually elaborated.

4.2 Humor Manager Configuration

The dialogue system is built accordingly to the proposition of (Young et al., 2010). More recent system architectures are available (most notably based on end-to-end recurrent neural networks) but it is not yet possible to bootstrap them without a training data set, which is our situation here. The system used hereafter has been trained in joint learning of semantic parser based on a zero-shot learning algorithm combined with the Q-learner RL approach to learn the dialogue manager policy. The humor manager policy is trained alongside the already trained dialogue policy. Ultimately it is foreseeable to train the two policies jointly but to reduce the state space we chose to fix the dialogue policy when learning the humor manager policies.

4.3 Results

To confirm the humor policy learning process, four profiles were defined and implemented in a user simulator. Each profile sets out a ratio of usage expected from each of the module: "uniform" (all modules and do-nothing are uniformly possible); "light" (all modules can only intervene less than 40% of the time, and are uniformly possible between each other); "jokes" (mainly jokes and do-nothing are possible, 30% and 40% respectively, and the others have low probabilities: 10%); "none" (no humor is allowed).

The user simulator tries to enforce these ratios in policy behaviours, but is also subject to the variability of the whole dialogue process and the availability of the various humor modules at each turn. Therefore the simulated trainings have been carried out to check how close the learned policy could be to the initial profiles. Each profile was used in 50 training simulations, of 500 epochs each. On a simulated test of 200 dialogue examples, without exploration, both "none" and "uniform" policies' distribution are almost identical to the definition of the profiles (exactly for "none" and less 1 point of difference for each type of humor for "uniform"). "Jokes" and "light" presents variations between 1 and 10 points.

The previous experiment only allowed us to confirm the adequacy between a user preference and a trained policy for humor usage. In a second step the whole system with humor generation mechanisms was tested in user trials. To this end, two profiles have been selected, "light" and "uniform," and their policy used in a system for a test of 124 dialogues each. 14 participants were recruited to evaluate the system with humor (they all tested the two profiles). They all already experimented the system in its baseline version, i.e. without humor. After each dialogue the users were prompted to answer a short survey with 6 questions :

- Success: "Was the task successful?" (0/1)
- System Understandability: "Was the system easy to understand?" [0,5]
- System Understanding: "Did the system understand you well?" [0,5]
- Humor Identification: "Do you think you identified when the system was making humor?" [0-5]
- Humor Impact: "Do you think humor had a favorable impact on your system perception?" [0-5]
- Humor Quantity: "Are you satisfied with the amount of humor produced by the system?" [0-5]

Table 1 shows the average results of the tests in user trials. Lines 1 to 3 display the overall number of tests, the success rate and the average cumulative rewards of the dialogue manager policy, respectively. The remaining lines provide the subjective scores made for each of the last 5 questions (task success is the first question). The integration of humor with the "light" or "uniform" profiles leads to very competitive success rates (83 % and 89 %) compared to what is observed without humor (86 %). These results, confirmed by the close values measured for the cumulative rewards for the three setups, show that humor does not disturb too much the dialogue system, especially since those differences were not significant[1]. There is also no significant[1] differences concerning the system understandability.

Interestingly, the judgments made over the understanding ability of the system are significantly[1] higher for the profiles with humor than the baseline, supporting the interest of introducing this social competence. Let us note that the use of the humor generation modules was easily identified by users (4.4 and 4.7/5). Finally, the last two questions with respect to the impact and quantity of humor show that judges do not really have a preference between the "light" and "uniform" profiles.

5 Conclusion

In this paper, several possibilities to integrate mechanisms to produce humorous utterances in an interactive artificial agent were introduced. A

[1]Statistical significances were analyzed with a two-tailed Welch's t-test. Results were considered statistically significant with a p-value < 0.001.

Model	No humor	"Light" profile	"Uniform" profile
Tests (#)	72	124	124
Success rate (%)	86	83	89
Average cumulative reward	10.2	9.8	10.7
System understandability	4.4	4.6	4.5
System understanding	2.6	3.3	3.5
Humor identification	—	4.4	4.7
Humor favorable impact	—	3.2	3.0
Humor quantity	—	3.5	3.5

Table 1: Evaluation of several profiles for humor generation policy.

two-step process has been devised. First, regular-enough humorous mechanisms have been identified, formalised and automated. Second, those mechanisms have been implemented in a dialogue system and their usage optimised by means of reinforcement learning and on-line adaptation learning approaches. To evaluate the social competence increase of artificial agents endowed with humor, evaluations with real users have been conducted. They allowed us to confirm that dialogue success rate is maintained at a comparable level while the system was generally judged more pleasant.

We have many other challenges ahead. The humor generation modules are in their initial states, and the user trials have been very instructive in highlighting several ways of improvements that will be pursued. Likewise, the optimisation process is currently limited to the nature and quantity of the generated humor. We are investigating an enlargement of the humor state so as to encompass more contextual information enabling the policy to react with greater opportunity.

Acknowledgments

This work has been partially carried out within the Labex BLRI (ANR-11-LABX-0036). The authors would like to thank Thomas Desfrançois for his contribution to this work.

References

Bryan Anthony Hong and Ethel Ong. 2009. Automatically Extracting Word Relationships as Templates for Pun Generation. In *NAACL HLT Workshop on Computational Approaches to Linguistic Creativity*, pages 24–31, Boulder, Colorado. Association for Computational Linguistics.

Kim Binsted and Graeme Ritchie. 1997. Computational rules for generating punning riddles. *Humor - International Journal of Humor Research*, 10(1).

Chiara Bucaria. 2004. Lexical and syntactic ambiguity as a source of humor: The case of newspaper headlines. *Humor*, 17(3):279–310.

Thierry Chaminade. 2017. An experimental approach to study the physiology of natural social interactions. *Interaction Studies*, 18(2):254–276.

Lucie Daubigney, Matthieu Geist, Senthilkumar Chandramohan, and Olivier Pietquin. 2012. A comprehensive reinforcement learning framework for dialogue management optimization. *Selected Topics in Signal Processing*, 6(8):891–902.

Thomas Desfrançois. 2016. Apprentissage automatique d'humour pour les système de dialogues vocaux (automatic learning of humor production for the vocal dialogue systems). Master Thesis.

Emmanuel Ferreira and Fabrice Lefèvre. 2015. Reinforcement-learning based dialogue system for human-robot interactions with socially-inspired rewards. *Computer Speech & Language*, 34(1):256–274.

Matthieu Geist and Olivier Pietquin. 2010. Managing uncertainty within value function approximation in reinforcement learning. In *Active Learning and Experimental Design workshop (collocated with AISTATS 2010)*, volume 92.

Dan Goldwasser and Xiao Zhang. 2016. Understanding Satirical Articles Using Common-Sense. *Transactions of the Association for Computational Linguistics*, 4:537–549.

Christian F Hempelmann, Victor Raskin, and Katrina E Triezenberg. 2006. Computer, Tell Me a Joke ... but Please Make it Funny: Computational Humor with Ontological Semantics. *FLAIRS Conference*.

Matthijs P Mulder and Antinus Nijholt. 2002. Humour Research: State of the Art. Technical report, University of Twente.

Andreea Niculescu, Betsy van Dijk, Anton Nijholt, Haizhou Li, and Swee Lan See. 2013. Making social robots more attractive: The effects of voice pitch, humor and empathy. *International Journal of Social Robotics*, 5(2):171–191.

Owen Rambow, Srinivas Bangalore, and Marilyn Walker. 2001. Natural language generation in dialog systems. In *HLT*.

Graeme Ritchie. 2005. Computational Mechanisms for Pun Generation. In *Proceedings of the 10th European Natural Language Generation Workshop*.

Graeme Ritchie. 2009. Can Computers Create Humor? *AI Magazine*, 30(3):71.

Steve Young, Milica Gašić, Simon Keizer, François Mairesse, Jost Schatzmann, Blaise Thomson, and Kai Yu. 2010. The hidden information state model: A practical framework for pomdp-based spoken dialogue management. *Computer Speech and Language*, 24(2):150–174.

Steve Young, Milica Gašić, Blaise Thomson, and Jason D. Williams. 2013. POMDP-based statistical spoken dialog systems: A review. *Proceedings of the IEEE*, 101(5):1160–1179.

Textual Entailment based Question Generation

Takaaki Matsumoto[1,2], **Kimihiro Hasegawa**[3], **Yukari Yamakawa**[1], and **Teruko Mitamura**[1]

[1]Carnegie Mellon University
[2]SOC Corporation
[3]Kobe University

{tmatsumo, yukariy, teruko}@andrew.cmu.edu, ljnjzbo417@gmail.com

Abstract

This paper proposes a novel question generation (QG) approach based on textual entailment. Many previous QG studies transform a single sentence into a question directly. They need hand-crafted templates or generate simple questions similar to the source texts. As a novel approach to QG, this research employs two-step QG: 1) generating new texts entailed by source documents, and 2) transforming the entailed sentences into questions. This process can generate questions that need the understanding of textual entailment to solve. Our system collected 1,367 English Wikipedia sentences as QG source, retrieved 647 entailed sentences from the web, and transformed them into questions. The evaluation result showed that our system successfully generated non-trivial questions based on textual entailment with 53% accuracy.

1 Introduction

Question generation (QG) is a practical application field of natural language generation. One important objective of QG in education is cultivating students' reading comprehension skills.

Many studies have been done on QG by transforming a single sentence into a question. Heilman and Smith (2010) researched QG based on syntactic parsing which is characterized by overgenerating and scoring. Mazidi and Tarau (2016) generated questions based on dependency parsing. Woo et al. (2016) studied QG based on dependency and semantic role labeling.

Their systems can generate relatively simple but grammatical questions. Suppose the following sentence is picked up from the website[1] .

1. *Kawabata won the Nobel Prize in Literature for his novel "Snow Country".*

Using the sentence above as a source, Heilman's system[2] generated the following question.

2. *Did Kawabata win the Nobel Prize in Literature for his novel "Snow Country"?*

Although this question is grammatical, its educational effectiveness could be minimized, since students might not exert their reading comprehension skills due to the similarity between the generated question and the original sentence. Questions generated by these QG methods are often quite similar to the original sentences.

Some researchers have tried inference QG with templates. Labutov et al. (2015) studied a QG system that utilizes ontology and templates developed by crowd workers. Chinkina and Meurers (2017) built a conceptual QG system using hand-crafted pattern matching templates. Although the templates in these studies may need more work, the generated questions are more complicated than those by transforming the single sentence.

Our research proposes a novel QG approach based on textual entailment. In contrast to the existing studies that directly generate questions from sources, our system firstly generates new sentences entailed by source texts and then transforms the entailed sentences into questions as shown in Figures 1 and 2. For example, we generate the following sentence entailed by the sentence (1).

3. *Kawabata is the writer of "Snow Country".*

Now we create a question for sentence (1) by transforming sentence (3) as follows.

[1]https://sites.google.com/site/ntcir11riteval/

[2]http://www.cs.cmu.edu/ ark/mheilman/questions/

Proceedings of the Workshop on Intelligent Interactive Systems and Language Generation (2IS&NLG), pages 15–19,
Tilburg, The Netherlands, November 5 2018.

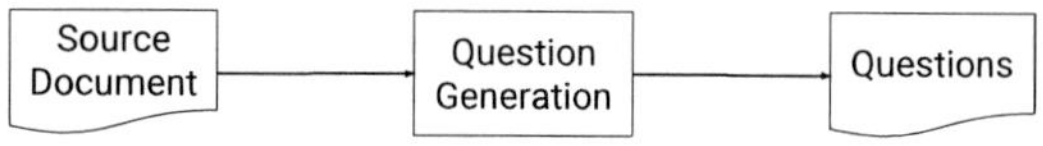

Figure 1: Existing QG Flow

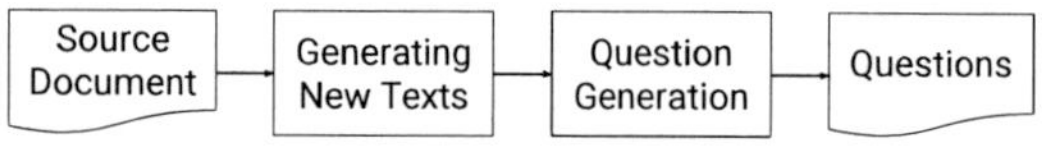

Figure 2: Proposed QG Flow

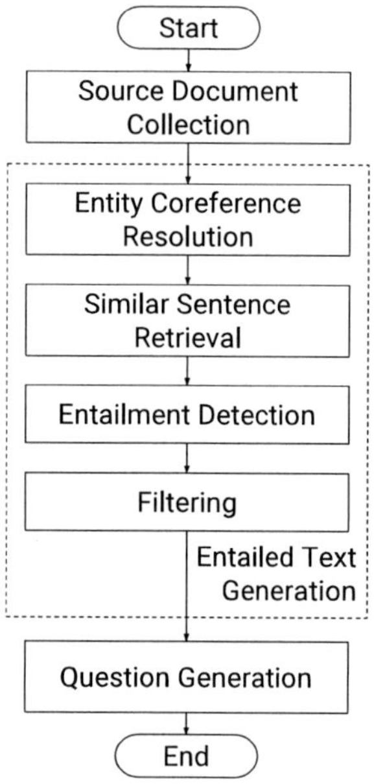

Figure 3: System Flow of the Proposed Approach

4. *Is Kawabata the writer of "Snow Country"?*

This question requires students to utilize more reading comprehension skills than the question (2), because there is not a word "writer" in the sentence (1). Students need to infer that Kawabata is a writer from the phrase of "won the Nobel Prize in Literature" in the sentence (1) using world knowledge. This method enables us to generate questions that are not similar to the original sentences but need textual entailment inference to solve.

2 Proposed Method

Figure 3 illustrates the QG process of this research. We first collected source texts. Second, we retrieved new texts entailed by the source sentences. Finally, we generated questions based on the entailed sentences. In the subsections below, we describe the function of each module.

2.1 Source Document Collection

Source texts for QG were collected from English Wikipedia. To generate entailed sentences for each source sentence, sentence tokenization using spaCy[3] was applied to all the collected sentences.

One example sentence from "Taj Mahal" article in English Wikipedia was the following:

5. *It is regarded by many as the best example of Mughal architecture and a symbol of India's rich history.*

2.2 Entailed Text Generation

We generate entailed texts by applying entailment detection to similar texts retrieved from the web.

2.2.1 Entity Coreference Resolution

To search texts similar to the collected sentences effectively, the entity coreferences of the source texts were resolved by using neuralcoref[4]. Coreferent entities are often important keywords to search similar sentences.

For example, the entity coreference of the sentence (5) was resolved as follows:

6. *The Taj Mahal is regarded by many as the best example of Mughal architecture and a symbol of India's rich history.*

2.2.2 Similar Sentence Retrieval

We then retrieved similar sentences from the web for each sentence with entity coreference resolved (for example, retrieving sentence (3) from sentence (1) in Section 1). In order to select sentences similar to the original text, we employed spaCy's sentence embedding to measure the similarity of sentences.

The following sentences are examples of the retrieved sentences for sentence (6) in this step.

7. *India, the Taj Mahal is by common consent the finest example of Mughal Architecture.*

8. *The Taj Mahal is considered one of the finest specimen of the Mughal architecture.*

9. *The Taj Mahal incorporates and expands on design traditions of Persian and earlier Mughal architecture.*

2.2.3 Entailment Detection

To extract entailed sentences from the similar retrieved sentences, we applied the ESMI entailment

[3]https://spacy.io

[4]https://github.com/huggingface/neuralcoref

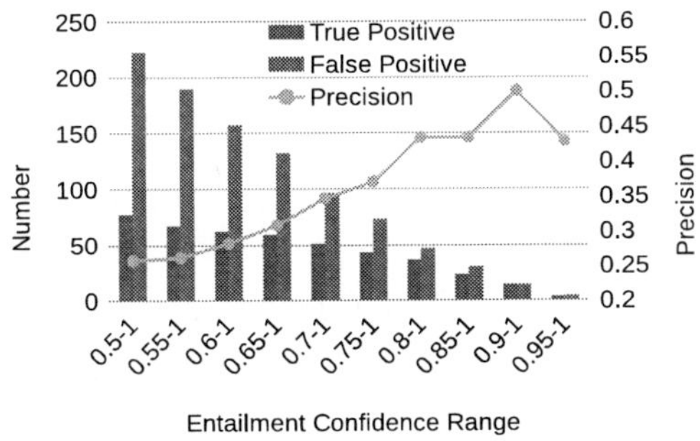

Figure 4: Preliminary Entailment Evaluation

Table 1: Filtering Values

	Min.	Max.
Entailment confidence	0.9	1
ROUGE-1	0.2	0.7
Sentence similarity	0.5	1
Num. of retrieved sentence words	6	-
Num. of source sentence words	Num. of retrieved sentence words	-

detector (Chen et al., 2017), which was trained using MultiNLI (Williams et al., 2018). We employed the GloVe (Pennington et al., 2014) as the word embedding for the ESIM.

For sentences (7), (8), and (9), the entailment detector labeled "entailment (confidence 0.93)," "entailment (confidence 0.60)," and "neutral (confidence 0.86)," respectively. Sentences (7) and (8) were kept because they were labeled as entailment. However, we eliminated sentence (9) because of the neutral label.

2.2.4 Filtering

Filtering was applied to improve the answer existence accuracy of the generated questions. Our filtering metrics include entailment confidence, ROUGE-1, sentence similarity, and the word counts of the source sentences and the retrieved ones. Table 1 shows the thresholds we used.

For sentences (7) and (8), sentence (7) was kept because it met all the criteria. However, sentence (8) was excluded because it did not satisfy the entailment confidence criterion.

Entailment Confidence Although the entailment detector can classify similar sentences retrieved, we filtered some results of entailment detection to increase the precision. Figure 4 shows the preliminary results of human evaluation. We collected Wikipedia sentences and retrieved the sentences labeled as "entailment" by the ESIM. As can be seen, the precision increases in proportion to the minimum threshold of the entailment confidence. To improve the entailment detector precision, we used a high confidence as a threshold.

ROUGE-1 To control the ratio of word overlapping between the entailed sentences and the source sentences, ROUGE-1 (Lin, 2004) was used.

Sentence Similarity We used spaCy to calculate sentence similarity between the source sentences and the entailed ones, because ROUGE-1 cannot measure semantic similarity.

The Word Counts of the Source Sentences and the Retrieved Ones We excluded too short sentences because they tend not to contain enough information.If a source sentence is too short, an entailed sentence would also be too short to make a question.

2.3 Question Generation

Questions based on textual entailment were generated by an existing QG tool. We chose Heilmen's QG system because it has been widely used as a baseline QG system in many papers (Woo et al. (2016) and Mazidi and Tarau (2016)). We picked up the top ranked yes/no question for each source sentence because Heilman's tool overgenerates questions.

For example, sentence (7) was transformed into the following question.

10. *Is the Taj Mahal by common consent the finest example of Mughal Architecture?*

3 Experiment

We collected 100 English Wikipedia abstracts as QG sources. We extracted 1,360 sentences by the sentence tokenization and their entity coreferences were resolved Then, we retrieved 61,330 similar sentences from the web (maximum 50 similar sentences per sentence). Maximum 30, 10 and 10 sentences were selected from the Google search results, English Wikipedia, and Simple Wikipedia, respectively. The entailment detector labeled 16,770 sentences as textual entailment with an argmax criterion, but 676 sentences remained after the filtering. We applied Heilman's QG system to them.

Answerable Examples:

1. Article: IQ

Source Sentence:

Unlike, for example, distance and mass, a concrete measure of intelligence cannot be achieved given the abstract nature of the concept of "intelligence".

H&S System's Yes/no Question:

Can distance and mass not be achieved given the abstract nature of the concept of ``intelligence'' for example?

Our System's Question:

Is it problematic to claim that the intelligence quotient is a measure of intelligence?

Retrieved Sentence:

So, it is problematic to claim that the intelligence quotient is a measure of intelligence.

2. Article: Classical economics

Source Sentence:

These economists produced a theory of market economies as largely self-regulating systems, governed by natural laws of production and exchange (famously captured by Adam Smith's metaphor of the invisible hand).

H&S System's Yes/no Question:

Were largely self-regulating systems governed by natural laws of production and exchange?

Our System's Question:

Is the invisible hand a natural force that self regulates the market economy?

Retrieved Sentence:

The invisible hand is a natural force that self regulates the market economy.

3. Article: Taj Mahal

Source Sentence:

It is regarded by many as the best example of Mughal architecture and a symbol of India's rich history.

H&S System's Yes/no Question:

(No yes/no questions were generated)

Our System's Question:

Is the Taj Mahal by common consent the finest example of Mughal Architecture?

Retrieved Sentence:

India, the Taj Mahal is by common consent the finest example of Mughal Architecture.

Unanswerable Examples:

1. Article: Castle

Source Sentence:

Many castles were originally built from earth and timber, but had their defences replaced later by stone.

H&S System's Yes/no Question:

Were many castles originally built from earth and timber?

Our System's Question:

Were castles?

Retrieved Sentence:

Castles, whether made of mortared stone or earth and timber, were.

Error: Similar sentence retrieval failure

2. Article: Hydrogen

Source Sentence:

Hydrogen is a chemical element with symbol H and atomic number 1.

H&S System's Yes/no Question:

Is hydrogen a chemical element with symbol H and atomic number 1?

Our System's Question:

Is Fermium a chemical element?

Retrieved Sentence:

Fermium (symbol Fm) is a chemical element.

Error: Entailment detection failure

3. Article: Measles

Source Sentence:

Measles is an airborne disease which spreads easily through the coughs and sneezes of infected people.

H&S System's Yes/no Question:

Is Measles an airborne disease which spreads easily through the coughs and sneezes of infected people?

Our System's Question:

Does coughs, or sneezes spread through the air?

Retrieved Sentence:

When an infected person breathes, coughs, or sneezes, the virus spreads through the air.

Error: Entailment was OK but question generation failed.

Figure 5: Examples of the Questions from Our System

3.1 Discussion

We evaluated 150 out of 676 generated questions. The evaluation results suggested that our system successfully generated textually entailed questions with 53% accuracy. Figure 5 lists answerable and unanswerable examples of the generated questions. Tables 2, 3, and 4 show the grammaticality, textual entailment, and answer existence of the evaluated questions, respectively.

The positive examples shown in Figure 5 suggests that the proposed method successfully generated relatively complex questions compared with Heilman's tool. In the first positive example, for instance, students need to infer that IQ is "problematic" to measure intelligence by the phrase of "a concrete measure of intelligence cannot be achieved" in the source sentence.

The questions from our system relatively shared a few number of words with the source sentences compared to questions directly generated from the source sentences by Heilman's tool. We measured two mean scores of ROUGE-1 (1) between the source texts and our system's questions, and (2) between the source texts and the questions generated directly from the source sentences by Heilman's tool. The mean scores of ROUGE-1 were 0.76 and 0.36, respectively. This difference suggests that the questions from our system would require more reading comprehension skills than the questions from Heilman's tool.

Table 2: Grammaticality of Questions

	Number	Ratio
Ungrammatical	26	0.17
Grammatical w/ minor errors	33	0.22
Grammatical	91	0.61

Table 3: Entailment of Retrieved Sentences

	Number	Ratio
Not Entailed	66	0.44
Entailed	84	0.56

Table 4: Answer Existence of Questions

	Number	Ratio
Unanswerable	70	0.47
Answerable	80	0.53

As can be seen in Table 2, about 83% of the evaluated questions were grammatical or grammatical with minor errors. Out of 26 ungrammatical questions, 14 were due to the errors of Heilman's system and 12 due to the errors in the retrieval process.

The evaluations of textual entailment and answer existence (Tables 3 and 4) were similar to each other because most of the unanswerable questions were generated from not-entailed sentences. However, there are a few exceptions. The retrieved text of the third unanswerable example in Figure 5 was entailed by the source text, but Heilman's tool generated an unanswerable question.

4 Conclusion

In this paper, a new question generation method using textually entailed information is proposed. We implemented the question generation system that utilizes textual entailment and applied it to English Wikipedia abstracts. For 1,367 source sentences, our system generated 647 questions and more than half of the evaluated questions were answerable. In the future, we plan to develop a natural language generation method to generate entailed sentences based on given texts instead of retrieving entailed sentences from the web.

Acknowledgements

The authors would like to acknowledge Dr. Jun Araki for his advice on this research. This publication was partly made possible by grant NPRP-08-1337-1-243 from the Qatar National Research Fund (a member of the Qatar Foundation). The statements made herein are solely the responsibility of the authors.

References

Qian Chen, Xiaodan Zhu, Zhenhua Ling, Si Wei, Hui Jiang, and Diana Inkpen. 2017. Enhanced lstm for natural language inference. In *Proceedings of the 55th Annual Meeting of the Association for Computational Linguistics (ACL 2017)*, Vancouver. ACL.

Maria Chinkina and Detmar Meurers. 2017. Question generation for language learning: From ensuring texts are read to supporting learning. In *Proceedings of the 12th Workshop on Innovative Use of NLP for Building Educational Applications*, pages 334–344.

Michael Heilman and Noah A Smith. 2010. Good question! statistical ranking for question generation. In *Human Language Technologies: The 2010 Annual Conference of the North American Chapter of the Association for Computational Linguistics*, pages 609–617. Association for Computational Linguistics.

Igor Labutov, Sumit Basu, and Lucy Vanderwende. 2015. Deep questions without deep understanding. In *Proceedings of the 53rd Annual Meeting of the Association for Computational Linguistics and the 7th International Joint Conference on Natural Language Processing (Volume 1: Long Papers)*, volume 1, pages 889–898.

Chin-Yew Lin. 2004. Rouge: A package for automatic evaluation of summaries. In *Text summarization branches out: Proceedings of the ACL-04 workshop*, volume 8. Barcelona, Spain.

Karen Mazidi and Paul Tarau. 2016. Infusing nlu into automatic question generation. In *Proceedings of the 9th International Natural Language Generation conference*, pages 51–60.

Jeffrey Pennington, Richard Socher, and Christopher D Manning. 2014. Glove: Global vectors for word representation. In *EMNLP*, volume 14, pages 1532–1543.

Adina Williams, Nikita Nangia, and Samuel Bowman. 2018. A broad-coverage challenge corpus for sentence understanding through inference. In *Proceedings of the 2018 Conference of the North American Chapter of the Association for Computational Linguistics: Human Language Technologies, Volume 1 (Long Papers)*, volume 1, pages 1112–1122.

Simon Woo, Zuyao Li, and Jelena Mirkovic. 2016. Good automatic authentication question generation. In *Proceedings of the 9th International Natural Language Generation conference*, pages 203–206.

Trouble on the Road: Finding Reasons for Commuter Stress from Tweets

Reshmi Gopalakrishna Pillai, Mike Thelwall and Constantin Orasan
Research Institute in Information and Language Processing
University of Wolverhampton, UK
reshmi.g85@gmail.com, {m.thelwall, c.orasan}@wlv.ac.uk

Abstract

Intelligent Transportation Systems could benefit from harnessing social media content to get continuous feedback. In this work, we implement a system to identify reasons for stress in tweets related to traffic using a word vector strategy to select a reason from a predefined list generated by topic modeling and clustering. The proposed system, which performs better than standard machine learning algorithms, could provide inputs to warning systems for commuters in the area and feedback for the authorities.

1 Introduction

Transportation systems connect hubs of human settlements and facilitate the movement of goods and people, with limiting congestion and accidents being a key design goal for cities. Continuous updates about traffic bottlenecks and accidents can help with this. The social web is a potential feedback source for transportation systems, providing insights about the experiences and mental states of commuters. Stress is a key factor to monitor since transportation problems of all kinds are likely to increase stress.

In this study, we implement a framework for finding the causes of stress expressed in tweets related to traffic. Our system identifies specific reasons for stress of commuters (accidents, congestion, etc.) that could be used to generate automated warnings for other travelers and feed in to context-aware GPS devices. Commuters can then take informed decisions to opt for alternate routes, avoiding traffic bottlenecks. Urban planning authorities can also leverage the analysis of stress reasons to take remedial actions as part of their Intelligent Transportation Systems strategy.

In this study we collected tweets about traffic in London during July 2018 and analyzed them to understand the reasons for the stress expressed by the commuters. As a pre-processing step, a list of potential stressors in the traffic domain was found by topic modelling and k-means clustering. Three different word-vector based methods were then applied to tweets to select a stressor from the stressors list. The output is evaluated by comparing it with the stress reason selected by human annotators.

The contributions of this work are as follows:

1. This is the first study detecting reasons for stress expressed in traffic-related tweets.
2. A dataset of traffic-related tweets annotated with reasons for stress.

2 Related Work

2.1 Stress Detection from Social Media

Social media has become a source of data for mental health analysis and evaluation. Lin et al. (2015) proposed a factor graph model combined with CNN based on linguistic, visual and social interaction data to detect stress from social media content. There have been several studies on detecting mental health disorders from social media data. De Choudhury et al. (2013a) leveraged behavioural patterns from social media, such as decreased activity, increased negative sentiment, religious involvement and clustered ego networks to build a classifier to proactively find the risk for depression in individuals before the onset. De Choudhury et al. (2013b) introduced a statistical model for predicting the onset of post-partum depression in mothers

Proceedings of the Workshop on Intelligent Interactive Systems and Language Generation (2IS&NLG), pages 20–25,
Tilburg, The Netherlands, November 5 2018.

with an accuracy of 71% using prenatal data and 80-83% when utilizing postnatal data as well. Also, the anonymity of mental health related postings in Reddit and online forums is an important factor which is discussed by Umashanthi (2015). Coppersmith et al. (2014) analysed linguistic features of Tweets of individuals with Post Traumatic Stress Disorder and built a classifier based on it. Stress can manifest around specific incidents, such as gun violence (Saha, 2017), and student deaths (Saha, 2018).

Thelwall et al. (2016) introduced TensiStrength, a novel lexicon-based system to detect stress/relaxation scores from social media based on linguistic resources such as LIWC (Tausczik and Pennebaker, 2010), General Inquirer (Stone et al, 1986) and the sentiment analysis software SentiStrength (Thelwall et al, 2010; Thelwall et al, 2012). Incorporation of word sense disambiguation (Gopalakrishna Pillai et al, 2018) improved the performance of TensiStrength.

Detecting reasons for stress from social media is a significant challenge. Lin et al. (2016) introduced a comprehensive scheme for identifying stressor event and subject and finding the stress reason and level based on it. This study is limited to personal stressor events, such as divorce, death, and relationships.

2.2 Natural Language Generation from Tweets

Traffic is a relatively new domain for the application of Natural Language Generation. However, with the proliferation of social media and accurate location devices, there is tremendous potential for data-driven, automatically generated messages about traffic incidents. Tran and Popowich (2016) introduced a novel generation model to provide location-relevant information. This traffic notification system trains a model to generate natural language texts and deliver real time warnings in case of traffic events.

Generating route descriptions is another application of NLG in traffic. Dale, Geldoff and Prost (2005) used GIS data as input and applies NLG principles to produce output texts. It used discourse structure to understand route structure and aggregation techniques to form fluent and natural sentences.

2.3 Analysis of traffic-related tweets

Lenormand et al. (2014) analyzed geo-located tweets from roads and railways in European countries. This study showed a positive correlation between the number of tweets and Average Annual Daily Traffic (AADT) on highways in France and the UK, especially in long highway segments.

Kurniawan et al. (2016) proposed tweets as an alternate source to detect traffic anomalies. Support Vector Machines achieved a classification accuracy of 99.77% in the task of detecting traffic events in Yogyakarta province in Indonesia. In a similar study, D'Andrea et al. (2015) implemented an SVM classification model to distinguish traffic from no-traffic tweets with an accuracy of 95.8% and to distinguish externally caused traffic events with an accuracy of 88.9%.

Long-term traffic prediction through tweet analysis has been shown to be effective by He et al. (2014) using traffic and Twitter data originating from San Francisco Bay in California. A cloud based system proposed by Sinnott and Yin (2015) has identified and verified accident black spots in the Australian city of Melbourne.

Gu, Cian and Chen (2016) discussed mining tweets as an inexpensive and novel way to find traffic incidents. Using a keyword dictionary, traffic incident tweets were identified, geocoded and then classified into one of five incident categories.

Cottrill and Gault (2017) analyzed a case study of a Twitter account @GamesTravel2014 used during the CommonWealth Games in Glasgow 2014, to share and respond to traffic related information. This Twitter account, in collaboration with the leading transportation providers in the city, was instrumental in detecting traffic hotspots. This case study establishes social media as a powerful tool to share trusted traffic information.

Salas and Georgakis (2017) created a collection of Tweets which mention traffic events in the UK. A key contribution of this work is a methodology with 88.27% accuracy for crawling, preprocessing and classifying traffic tweets using Natural Language Processing and Support Vector Machines. The dataset was analyzed to find the temporal and linguistic features of the Tweets.

Lv and Chen (2016) summarized the main research topics in transportation research using social media. However, though traffic-related tweets have been studied for identification of traffic events, the sentiments of the commuters using transportation systems have been largely unexplored. Cao and

Zeng (2014) proposed Traffic Sentiment Analysis as a new tool to analyze sentiments expressed in traffic related social media content. In the context of the 'yellow light rule' and fuel prices in China, they demonstrated the architecture, data collection and process of their methods. Our system is the first attempt to identify stress reasons in the social media outputs of commuters, providing feedback about the improvement areas for transportation systems.

3 Methodology

We use a two-step method developed in our earlier research on finding stress reasons for airlines and politics (Gopalakrishna Pillai et al., 2018b). High-stress tweets belonging to the traffic domain were first analyzed by topic modelling to find the most frequently occurring topics. A list of potential reasons for stress in traffic was constructed from it. In the second step, tweets were analyzed by word-vector methods to find the reason for stress from the potential list.

3.1 Overview

Construction of Potential Stressors list: Our study was limited to tweets discussing traffic in the city of London. The tweets collected were preprocessed by removing duplicates. They were assigned stress scores by TensiStrength, on a scale of -1 to -5, (-1 denote the least stress and -5 the highest stress).

The higher stress scored Tweets (with score -5 or -4) constituted the corpus for performing batch-wise LDA topic modeling with hashtag pooling. The topics from this step were grouped into 5 clusters(the number of clusters was chosen based on the coherence of the collection).

A label was assigned to each cluster using the most similar word vector method. These cluster labels encasing the most frequent topics in high-stress tweets constituted the potential stressors for the traffic domain (Table 1).

Example topics in the cluster	Stressor
Air cleanair smoke fog burning noise emissions mess	Pollution
Accident damage collision break-down fatality	accident
Race hour rush delay late hours slow jam busy mayhem chocker	Congestion
Attack assault gunman fear chaos kill crime murder terrorist blast stab	Violence
Awareness counsel protest march rally public crowd	Campaign

Table 1: Clusters and stressors (London Traffic)

Finding stress reasons for tweets: As previously introduced for politics and airlines (Gopalakrishna Pillai et al., 2018b), we employed 3 word-vector based methods to find causes for stress in Tweets.

Method 1 (maximum word similarity): Select the stressor with the highest cosine similarity with any of the content words in the tweets.

Method 2 (context vector similarity): Select the stressor with the highest cosine similarity with the context vector representing the tweet (average of vectors corresponding to the content words).

Method 3 (cluster vector similarity): This is the same as Method 2, but the stressor is represented by a cluster vector found by averaging vectors of all words in the topic cluster. Select the cluster with highest cosine similarity with the context vector.

3.2 Dataset and Annotation

We first collected 23249 tweets from 1st to 31st July 2018 with the Twitter API. The search queries were strings and hashtags related to traffic in London and two key motorways ('London' AND 'traffic', #london AND #traffic, #londontraffic, #m25, #m40). Removing tweets consisting only of URLs, and duplicate tweets, left 13321 tweets. Using TensiStrength, these tweets were given scores in a scale of -1 to -5 to indicate their stress level. There were 2334 tweets with a stress score of -4 or -5. A high-stress traffic tweet corpus was created by randomly selecting the 1000 tweets from this set. This was divided into 5 groups with 200 tweets each and each group was subjected to LDA-based topic modelling with hashtag pooling. A list of potential stressors in the traffic domain was created as described in the previous section.

Out of the 4410 tweets with -5, -4 or -3 stress scores, the 1000 tweets which were used for finding the potential stress reasons were excluded and from the remaining tweets, 2000 were randomly chosen for evaluation of the word vector methods. We included Tweets with stress score -3 too in this dataset because this is a sufficiently high stress score for the annotators and the word vector analysis to assign a stress reason.

These 2000 tweets were annotated individually and independently by three human coders, marking them with the most appropriate reason for stress from the list of potential stressors. The annotators had engaged in a similar stress-reason annotation experiment, and their reliability was further assessed with Krippendorff's α inter-coder agreement scores. The agreement rates were sufficiently high to claim that the annotations are coherent and usable (Table 2).

Agreement Between Coders	**Krippendorff's α**
A and B	0.732
B and C	0.786
A and B	0.721

Table 2: Inter-coder agreement for stressor annotation (London Traffic)

3.3 Experimental Setup

The experiments performed were similar to our earlier research on finding stress reasons for airlines and politics (Gopalakrishna Pillai et al., 2018b). To train the word vectors for finding stressors, we used a Word2Vec model trained on 400 million tweets, from an ACL WNUT task (Godin et al, 2015).

The default Weka 3.6 configurations of three machine learning algorithms (AdaBoost: An adaptive boosting algorithm, Logistic Regression and Support Vector Machines) were run using 10-fold cross validation to serve as comparison baselines for our methods. The feature selection was adapted from a similar task of assessing the stress and relaxation strengths expressed in tweets (Thelwall, 2017). Term unigrams, bigrams and trigrams and their frequencies were used as features. Punctuation was included as a term, with consecutive punctuation treated as a single term.

4 Results

4.1 Results Summary

The stress reasons for the traffic tweets were found using the word vector processing methods. It is summarized in Table 3. Cluster vector method gives the best performance in terms of precision, recall and accuracy.

Figure 1 shows a distribution of stress reasons in the traffic Tweets.

Method	**Percentage Correct**	**Precision**	**Recall**
max. word	48.3%	47.6%	46.3
context vector	53.9%	52.1%	52.5%
cluster vector	**63.8%**	**62.3%**	**61.4%**
SVM	50.1%	52.2%	55.7%
AdaBoost	52.5%	54.3%	52.8%
Logistic	49.7%	43.6%	48.7%

Table 3: Accuracy of stress reason detection methods applied to London Traffic tweets

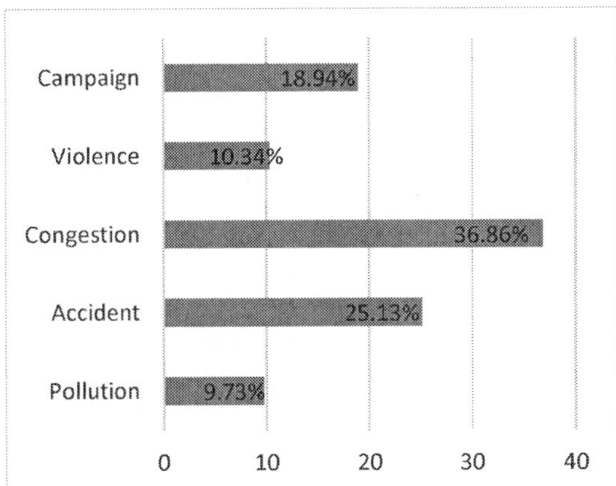

Figure 1: Stress reasons detected in London Traffic Tweets by the cluster vector method

4.2. Error Analysis

Indirect/Sarcastic Expressions: Tweets with an indirect expressions of stress pose a challenge to our methods. An example is "The joys of London traffic; not moving for last one hour is killing me", "Lea Bridge rd E10 traffic is murder really London counsel" in which the reason for stress is Congestion, but is detected as violence.

Multiple stressors: Tweets in which there are multiple reasons for stress. E.g.: "Vehicle emissions rise during rush hours, making the traffic jams hellish" has two stressors, "pollution" and "congestion". A possible solution will be to expand the methods to accommodate multiple stressors.

5 Conclusion and Future Work

This paper proposed and implemented word vector based methods to find the reasons for stress expressed in Traffic domain. A dataset containing 23249 Tweets about London traffic were collected and after preprocessing, 2000 tweets were randomly chosen to be annotated by human coders for the reasons for stress. The performance of our proposed methods to detect the reasons for stress in this dataset was compared to that of standard machine learning algorithms. As a future work, we propose to extend this study to content in other social media and to modify our methods to accommodate Tweets with multiple stressors.

This automated stress detection from tweets can identify traffic bottlenecks and accident-prone areas. These reasons identified for traffic-related stress can be used as inputs in the form of pictograms or short texts to an automated warning system for the commuters and feedback for the traffic policymakers. Further research is required to use the findings of this stress reason detection method for improving Intelligent Transportation Systems.

Acknowledgement

This research was supported by the European Union's Horizon 2020 research and innovation programme under grant agreement No 636160-2, the Optimum project www.optimumproject.eu.

References

Jianping Cao et al., "Web-Based Traffic Sentiment Analysis: Methods and Applications," in IEEE Transactions on Intelligent Transportation Systems, vol. 15, no. 2, pp. 844-853, April 2014. doi: 10.1109/TITS.2013.2291241

Glen A. Coppersmith, Craig T. Harman, and Mark Dredze. 2014. Measuring post traumatic stress disorder in Twitter. In Proceedings of the International AAAI Conference on Weblogs and Social Media (ICWSM).

Caitlin Cottrill, Paul Gault, Godwin Yeboah, John D. Nelson, Jillian Anable, Thomas Budd, Tweeting Transit: An examination of social media strategies for transport information management during a large event, Transportation Research Part C: Emerging Technologies, Volume 77, 2017, Pages 421-432, ISSN 0968-090X, https://doi.org/10.1016/j.trc.2017.02.008.

Robert Dale and Sabine Geldof and Jean-Philippe Prost. (2005). Using Natural Language Generation

in Automatic Route Description. Journal of Research and Practice in Information Technology. 37.

Eleonora D'Andrea, Pietro Ducange, Beatrice Lazzerini, Francesco Marcelloni "Real-Time Detection of Traffic From Twitter Stream Analysis," in IEEE Transactions on Intelligent Transporta-tion Systems, vol. 16, no. 4, pp. 2269-2283, Aug. 2015. doi: 10.1109/TITS.2015.2404431

Munmun De Choudhury, Michael Gamon, Scott Counts, and Eric Horvitz. 2013a. Predicting depression via social media. In Proceedings of the International AAAI Conference on Weblogs and Social Media (ICWSM).

Munmun De Choudhury, Scott Counts, Eric Horvitz, 2013b. Predicting Postpartum Changes in Behavior and Mood via Social Media. In Proc. CHI 2013, to appear.

Reshmi Gopalakrishna Pillai, Mike Thelwall, Constantin Orasan. 2018a. Detection of Stress and Relaxation Magnitudes for Tweets. In The 2018 Web Conference Companion (WWW'18 Com-panion), April 23-27, 2018, Lyon, France, ACM, New York, NY, 8 pages. DOI: https://doi.org/10.1145/3184558.3191627

Reshmi Gopalakrishna Pillai, Mike Thelwall, Constantin Orasan, 2018b. What Makes you Stressed? Finding Reasons From Tweets. Proceedings of the 9th Workshop on Computational Approaches to Subjectivity, Sentiment & Social Media Analysis, EMNLP-2018.

Yiming Gu, Zhen Qian, Feng Chen From twitter to detector: real-time traffic incident detection using social media data. Transport. Res. Part C: Emerging Technol., 67 (2016), pp. 321-342

Jingrui He, Wei Shen, Phani Divakaruni, Laura Wynter and Rick Lawrence. "Improving Traffic Prediction with Tweet Semantics." IJCAI (2013).

Dwi Aji Kurniawan, Sunu Wibirama and Noor Akhmad Setiawan, "Real-time traffic classifica-tion with Twitter data mining," 2016 8th Interna-tional Conference on Information Technology and Electrical Engineering (ICITEE), Yogyakar-ta, 2016, pp. 1-5.doi: 10.1109/ICITEED.2016.7863251

Maxim Lenormand, Antonia Tugores, Pere Colet, Jose J Ramasco (2014) Tweets on the Road. PLoS ONE 9(8): e105407. https://doi.org/10.1371/journal.pone.0105407

Huijie Lin, Jia Jia, Jiezhong Qui, Yongfeng Zhang, Guangyao Shen, Lexing Xie, Jie Tan, Ling Feng, Tat-Seng Chua. Detecting stress based on social interactions in social networks. 2017. IEEE Transactions on Knowledge and Data Engineering, 2017.

Huijie lin, Jia Jia, Lexing Xie, Guangyao Shen, Tat-Seng Chua. 2016. What does social media say about your stress? In Proceedings of the Twenty-Fifth International Joint Conference on Artificial Intelligence,3775–3781.

Yisheng Lv, Yuangyuang Chen, Xiqiao Zhang, Yanjie Duan and Naiqiang L. Li, "Social media based transportation research: the state of the work and the networking," in IEEE/CAA Journal of Automatica Sinica, vol. 4, no. 1, pp. 19-26, Jan. 2017. doi: 10.1109/JAS.2017.7510316

Umashanthi Pavalanathan and Munmun De Choudhury. 2015. Identity Management and Mental Health Discourse in Social Media. In Proceedings of the 24th International Conference on World Wide Web (WWW '15 Companion). ACM, New York, NY, USA, 315-321. DOI: https://doi.org/10.1145/2740908.2743049

Koustuv Saha, and Munmun De Choudhury. 2017. Modeling stress with social media around incidents of gun violence on college campuses.

Koustuv Saha, Ingmar Weber and Munmun De Choudhury. 2018. A Social Media Based Examination of the Effects of Counseling Recommendations After Student Deaths on College Campuses.

Angelica Salas, Panagiotis Georgakis, C. Nwagboso, Ahmad Ammari and Ionnis Petalas, "Traffic event detection framework using social media," 2017 IEEE International Conference on Smart Grid and Smart Cities (ICSGSC), Singapore, 2017, pp. 303-307. doi: 10.1109/ICSGSC.2017.8038595

Richard Sinnott, Yikai Gong & Fengmin Deng (2015). Identification of (near) Real-time Traffic Congestion in the Cities of Australia through Twitter. 7-12. 10.1145/2811271.2811276.

Philip J. Stone, Dexter C. Dunphy, Marshall S. Smith and Daniel M. Ogilvie. 1966. The general inquirer: A computer approach to content analy-sis. Cambridge, MA: The MIT Press.

Yla R. Tausczik and James W. Pennebaker, 2010. The psychological meaning of words: LIWC and computerized text analysis methods. Journal of language and social psychology, 29(1), 24-54.

Mike Thelwall, Kevan Buckley Georgios Paltoglou, D. Cai and A. Kappas. 2010. Sentiment strength detection in short informal text. Journal of the American Society for Information Science and Technology, 61(12), 2544–2558.

Mike Thelwall, Kevan Buckley, and Georgios Pal-toglou. 2012. Sentiment strength detection for the social web. J. Am. Soc. Inf. Sci. Technol. 63, 1 (January 2012), 163-173. DOI=http://dx.doi.org/10.1002/asi.21662

Mike Thelwall. 2017. TensiStrength: stress and re-laxation magnitude detection for social media texts. Journal of Information Processing and Management. 53: 106–121

Khoa Tran and Fred Popowich, Automatic Tweet Generation From Traffic Incident Data, Proceedings of the 2nd International Workshop on Natural Language Generation and the Semantic Web (WebNLG 2016), 2016, Association for Computational Linguistics, 59-66.

Assisted Nominalization for Academic English Writing

John Lee[1,2], Dariush Saberi[1], Marvin Lam[3], Jonathan Webster[1,2]
[1] Department of Linguistics and Translation, City University of Hong Kong
[2] The Halliday Centre for Intelligent Applications of Language Studies, City University of Hong Kong
[3] Department of English, The Hong Kong Polytechnic University
jsylee@cityu.edu.hk, dsaberi2-c@my.cityu.edu.hk,
marvin.lam@polyu.edu.hk, ctjjw@cityu.edu.hk

Abstract

Nominalization is a common linguistic feature in academic writing. By expressing actions or events (verbs) as concepts or things (nouns), nominalization produces more abstract and formal text, and conveys a more objective tone. We report our progress in developing a system that offers automatic assistance for nominalization. Given an input sentence with a complex clause, it paraphrases the sentence into a simplex clause by transforming verb phrases into noun phrases. Preliminary evaluations suggest that system performance achieved high recall.

1 Introduction

University students who are non-native speakers of English often experience significant difficulties in studying content subjects in English, due in large part to their problems with academic writing (Evans and Green, 2007). The traditional focus in computer-assisted language learning and natural language processing has been the development of algorithms for correcting grammatical errors (Dahlmeier et al., 2013) and improving sentence fluency (Sakaguchi et al., 2016). The focus of this paper, in contrast, is to help students improve their writing style in Academic English.

Our long-term goal is to help students make use of the full range of options available along what M. A. K. Halliday calls the cline of metaphoricity (Halliday and Matthiessen, 2014). This cline ranges between the clausally complex, lexically simple congruent construal of experience at one end, and the clausally simple, lexically dense metaphorical re-construal at other end. Table 1 shows paraphrases of an example sentence along this cline. We envision a system that provides assistance in moving a sentence from any point on the cline to another. As a first step towards this goal, the current system focuses on paraphrasing a complex clause (e.g., "Because she didn't know the rules, she died.") into a simplex clause ("Her ignorance of the rules caused her to die.").

The rest of the paper is organized as follows. The next section summarizes previous work in automatic paraphrasing. Section 3 describes the three components in our system: syntactic parser, nominalizer, and sentence generator. Section 4 evaluates system performance, focusing on the output of the nominalizer. Section 5 concludes and discusses future work.

2 Previous work

Previous work in automatic paraphrasing can be viewed at two levels. At the word level, research in lexical substitution (McCarthy and Navigli, 2009) and the related task of lexical simplification (Specia et al., 2012) aims to replace a word or short phrase with another, while preserving the meaning of the original sentence.

At the sentence level, most previous work focused on syntactic simplification, i.e., to reduce the syntactic complexity of a sentence by splitting a complex sentence into two or more simple sentences (Siddharthan, 2002). In terms of the cline of metaphoricity, then, it transforms a "complex clause" into a "cohesive sequence" (Table 1). Typically, the system analyzes the input sentence via a parse tree, applies manually written transformation rules (Bott et al., 2012; Siddharthan and Angrosh, 2014; Saggion et al., 2015), and then performs sentence re-generation. Our system adopts a similar architecture and also takes a complex clause as input, but works in the opposite direction on the cline: it attempts to transform the complex clause into a simplex clause.

Proceedings of the Workshop on Intelligent Interactive Systems and Language Generation (2IS&NLG), pages 26–30,
Tilburg, The Netherlands, November 5 2018.

Domain	**System**	**Example**
Cohesive sequence	conjunction	She didn't know the rules. Consequently, she died.
Complex clause	parataxis hypotaxis	She didnt know the rules; so she died. Because she didnt know the rules, she died.
Simplex clause	causation circumstantiation relational process	Her ignorance of the rules caused her to die. Through ignorance of the rules, she died. Her death was due to ignorance of the rules. Her ignorance of the rules caused her death. The cause of her death was her ignorance of the rules.
Nominal group	qualification	Her death through ignorance of the rules.

Table 1: The cline of metaphoricity, illustrated with example paraphrases of a sentence expressing a relationship of cause (Halliday and Matthiessen, 2014).

Component	**Example**
Input	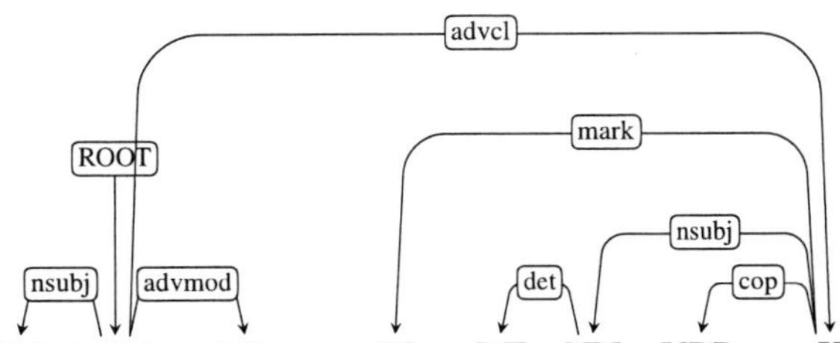 POS tag: PRP VBD RB IN DT NN VBD JJ Word: She died suddenly because the doctor was negligent
Syntactic Parser	Main clause = "She died suddenly" Subordinate clause = "The doctor was negligent" Linking word = "because"
Nominalizer	NP for main clause = "her sudden death" NP for subordinate clause = "the doctor's negligence"
Sentence Generator	"The doctor's negligence caused her sudden death."

Table 2: The system extracts the main and subordinate clauses of the input sentence with the *Syntactic Parser* (Section 3.1); (2) transforms the clauses into noun phrases with the *Nominalizer* (Section 3.2); and (3) links the noun phrases to produce a sentence with the *Sentence Generator* (Section 3.3).

3 Approach

Our system is a pipeline with three components (Table 2).

3.1 Syntactic parser

Given an input sentence, we use the SpaCy dependency parser (Honnibal and Johnson, 2015) to derive its syntactic tree in Universal Dependencies (Nivre et al., 2016). The system determines whether a sentence contains a complex clause by searching for the adverbial clause modifier (`advcl`) relation. If so, the system extracts the main clause from the head word of the `advcl` relation, the subordinate clause from its child word, and the linking word from the `mark` relation. In Table 2, for example, it extracts "She died suddenly" as the main clause, "the doctor was negligent" as the subordinate clause, and "because" as the linking word.

3.2 Nominalizer

Given a clause with a verb phrase, the Nominalizer matches its tree structure to the pattern shown in Table 3. It then transforms the clause into a noun phrase with the following steps:

- Identify the main verb (`verb`) and generate its nominalized form, $v2n$(`verb`). In the example in Table 3, "died" is transformed into "death". We do not treat verbs-to-be, modal

Input	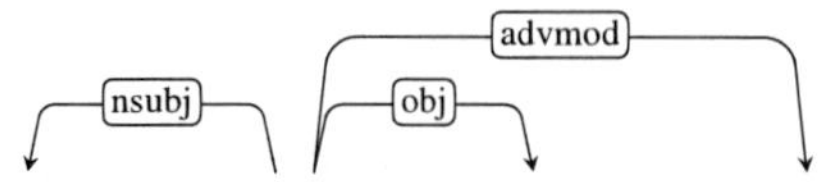 POS tag: N* V* N* RB Word: noun verb $noun_{obj}$ adv ↓ ↓ ↓ *gen*(noun) *v2n*(verb) $noun_{obj}$ *adv2adj*(adv) Example: She died suddenly ↓ ↓ ↓ her death sudden
Output	*gen*(noun) *adv2adj*(adv) *v2n*(verb) of $noun_{obj}$ (Example: "her sudden death") the *adv2adj*(adv) *v2n*(verb) of noun the *adv2adj*(adv) *v2n*(verb) of $noun_{obj}$ by noun

Table 3: Nominalization rule, where $v2n$ is the mapping from a verb to a noun; $adv2adj$ is the mapping from an adverb to an adjective; and gen is the mapping from a nominative noun to its genitive form.

verbs and negated verbs, since their nominalization patterns vary considerably depending on meaning and context.

- Identify the adverb (adv), if any, and generate its adjectival form, *adv2adj*(adv). For example, "suddenly" is transformed into "sudden" in Table 3.
- Identify the direct object ($noun_{obj}$) and prepositional phrases, if any, and place them after the nominalized main verb.
- Identify the subject (noun). If the subject is a pronoun or a short noun, use the first output template in Table 3. For pronouns, *gen*(noun) generates its possessive form (e.g., "she" → "her"); for nouns, it appends a possessive apostrophe (e.g., "doctor" → "doctor's"). For longer noun phrases, the system prepends "of" when using the second template, or "by" when using the third template (e.g., "the doctor in the clinic" → "of/by the doctor in the clinic").

A similar rule is defined for clauses with an adjectival phrase (e.g., "The doctor was negligent"). Using an adjective-to-noun mapping $adj2n$, it rewrites the adjective into a noun (e.g., "the doctor's negligence"). Both rules operate on the following part-of-speech conversion lists:

Verb-to-noun ($v2n$) We constructed our verb-to-noun list based on the NOM entries[1] from NOMLEX (Meyers et al., 1998). For verbs not covered by NOMLEX, we retrieved their nouns in CATVAR (Habash and Dorr, 2003). When a verb is mapped to multiple nouns, we choose the one with the highest unigram frequency count in the *Google Web 1T Corpus* (Brants and Franz, 2006) that ends with a typical noun suffix[2]. This procedure yielded 7,879 one-to-one verb-noun mappings.

Adjective-to-noun ($adj2n$) We constructed our adjective-to-noun list with a similar procedure based on the NOMADJ entries from NOMLEX and verb-adjective pairs in CATVAR. There are 11,369 unique one-to-one adjective-noun mappings.

Adverb-to-adjective ($adv2adj$) We constructed our adverb-to-adjective mapping with CATVAR, with a total of 2,834 such mappings.

The current system assumes one-to-one mappings for the above, though it is clear that polysemy necessitates one-to-many mappings. For example, the verb "descend" should be nominalized as "descendance" in the context of "descendance from royalty", but as "descent" in the context of "descent from the mountain". In future work, we plan to incorporate automatic semantic disambiguation to make this distinction.

[1]We excluded the NOMLIKE entries, and those whose NOM-TYPE is SUBJECT, e.g., "teacher" for the verb "teach".

[2]'-age', '-ance', '-ce', '-cy', '-dge', '-dom', '-ence', '-ery', '-ess', '-esse', '-hood', '-ice', '-ics', '-ion', '-ise', '-ism', '-ity', '-ment', '-ry', '-ship', '-th', '-tude', '-ty', '-ure'.

3.3 Sentence Generator

The Sentence Generator takes as input the noun phrases produced by the Nominalizer for the main clause and subordinate clause. It then recombines them into a complete sentence based on the semantic relation between them. Since implicit discourse identification remains a challenging task (Braud and Denis, 2014), the system determines the relation by keyword spotting; the keywords "because", "since", "so", and "therefore" for the causal relation; "although", "despite", "even though" for the concession relation, "after", "before" for the temporal relation, etc. In Table 2, the system infers the relation as causal based on the keyword "because", and links the two noun phrases with the verb "to cause" ("The doctor's negligence caused her sudden death"). In other contexts, another linking word may be warranted, such as "to result in", "to lead to", "to be due/attributable to", "to be a result of", "to lie in" etc. Currently, our system lets the user choose the most appropriate word.

4 Evaluation

We performed a preliminary evaluation that focuses on the Nominalizer. We first describe our dataset and metric (Section 4.1), and then discuss the results (Section 4.2).

4.1 Data and evaluation metric

Our test data included 33 clauses present in 25 sentences from Wikipedia, covering causal, concession, and temporal relations. To produce the gold annotation, we asked a senior staff member at the English Language Centre at our university to rewrite these sentences in more nominalized forms, using a simplex clause whenever possible.

We applied our system on these sentences, and classified the system output into three categories:

- *Identical* to the gold annotation other than the position of the subject. For example, the two NPs "the existence of the company" and "the company's existence" would be considered identical;
- *Minor revision*, i.e., same choice of nominalized verb or adjective, but different choices for determiners or prepositions elsewhere in the NP. For example, the two NPs "a decrease in the number" versus "the decrease in the number" would fall into this category;
- *Major revision*, i.e., different choice of nominalized verb or adjective.

4.2 Results

While our system attempted nominalization for all 33 clauses, the human annotator nominalized only 18 of them. This suggests that in the other 15 cases, the system offered nominalizations that resulted in a less fluent sentence.

Among clauses that should be nominalized, the system achieved relatively high recall. Out of the 18 nominalizations, the system output is identical in 55.6%; requires minor revision in 16.7%; and major revision in 27.8%. Minor revisions were caused by subtle abstractions that are produced by nominalization. For example, the clause "(... even though) the years passed" was nominalized as "the passage of years" in the gold annotation, while the system did not delete the definite article. Major revisions were due sometimes to a less fluent choice of noun. For instance, "they are wrong ..." was paraphrased as "their error" in the gold annotation, while the system more mechanically generated "their wrongness". In other cases, they reflected different paraphrasing strategies. For example, the annotator nominalized "the stem is nice because ..." as "... is an attractive feature of the stem", rather than directly using a nominalized form of "nice".

5 Conclusion

We have presented a system that assists users in improving their Academic English by suggesting nominalizations. It applies transformation rules on dependency parse trees, and performs nominalization using two existing resources, NOMLEX (Meyers et al., 1998) and CATVAR (Habash and Dorr, 2003). Preliminary evaluations suggest that the system has high recall but low precision: when a clause can indeed be nominalized, the system is able to offer valid suggestions; it also provides suggestions, however, that would yield less natural sentences. As such, it is currently suitable for more advanced students who can judge the quality of these suggestions.

We plan to pursue three lines of research in future work. First, we hope to construct better verb-to-noun and adjective-to-noun mappings with automatic sense disambiguation. Second, we aim to raise precision by detecting sentences that are not amenable to nominalization. Finally, we plan to train the sentence generator to rank its suggestions of words for linking the noun phrases.

Acknowledgments

The work was partially funded by a CityU-led Teaching and Learning Project in the 2016-19 Triennium (Title of the project: Meeting the Challenge of Teaching and Learning Language in the University: enhancing linguistic competence and performance in English and Chinese) from the University Grants Committee.

References

Stefan Bott, Horacio Saggion, and David Figueroa. 2012. A Hybrid System for Spanish Text Simplification. In *Proc.Workshop on Speech and Language Processing for Assistive Technologies*.

Thorsten Brants and Alex Franz. 2006. The google web 1t 5-gram corpus version 1.1. In *LDC2006T13*.

Chloé Braud and Pascal Denis. 2014. Combining Natural and Artificial Examples to Improve Implicit Discourse Relation Identification. In *Proc. COLING*.

Daniel Dahlmeier, Hwee Tou Ng, and Siew Mei Wu. 2013. Building a Large Annotated Corpus of Learner English: The NUS Corpus of Learner English. In *Proc. 8th Workshop on Innovative Use of NLP for Building Educational Applications*.

Stephen Evans and Christopher Green. 2007. Why EAP is Necessary: A Survey of Hong Kong Tertiary Students. *Journal of English for Academic Purposes*, 6(1):3–17.

Nizar Habash and Bonnie Dorr. 2003. A Categorial Varation Database for English. In *Proc. NAACL*.

M. A. K. Halliday and C. M. I. M. Matthiessen. 2014. *Hallidays Introduction to Functional Grammar*. Routledge.

Matthew Honnibal and Mark Johnson. 2015. An Improved Non-monotonic Transition System for Dependency Parsing. In *Proc. EMNLP*.

Diana McCarthy and Roberto Navigli. 2009. The English Lexical Substitution Task. *Language Resources and Evaluation*, 43:139–159.

Adam Meyers, Catherine Macleod, Roman Yangarber, Ralph Grishman, Leslie Barrett, and Ruth Reeves. 1998. Using nomlex to produce nominalization patterns for information extraction. In *Proc. Computational Treatment of Nominals*.

Joakim Nivre, Marie-Catherine de Marneffe, Filip Ginter, Yoav Goldberg, Jan Hajic, Christopher D. Manning, Ryan McDonald, Slav Petrov, Sampo Pyysalo, Natalia Silveira, Reut Tsarfaty, and Daniel Zeman. 2016. Universal Dependencies v1: A Multilingual Treebank Collection. In *Proc. Tenth International Conference on Language Resources and Evaluation (LREC)*.

Horacio Saggion, Sanja Štajner, Stefan Bott, Simon Mille, Luz Rello, and Biljana Drndarevic. 2015. Making It Simplext: Implementation and Evaluation of a Text Simplification System for Spanish. *ACM Transactions on Accessible Computing (TACCESS)*, 6(4).

Keisuke Sakaguchi, Courtney Napoles, Matt Post, and Joel Tetreault. 2016. Reassessing the Goals of Grammatical Error Correction: Fluency Instead of Grammaticality. *Transactions of the Association for Computational Linguistics*.

Advaith Siddharthan. 2002. An Architecture for a Text Simplification System. In *Proc. Language Engineering Conference (LEC)*.

Advaith Siddharthan and M. A. Angrosh. 2014. Hybrid Text Simplification using Synchronous Dependency Grammars with Hand-written and Automatically Harvested Rules. In *Proc. EACL*.

Lucia Specia, Sujay Kumar Jauhar, and Rada Mihalcea. 2012. SemEval-2012 Task 1: English Lexical Simplification. In *Proc. First Joint Conference on Lexical and Computational Semantics (*SEM)*.

Two-Step Training and Mixed Encoding-Decoding for Implementing a Generative Chatbot with a Small Dialogue Corpus

Jintae Kim[1], **Hyeon-Gu Lee**[1], **Harksoo Kim**[1], **Yeonsoo Lee**[2] and **Young-Gil Kim**[3]

[1]Kangwon National University Computer and Communication Engineering, Korea
[2]NCSOFT Corp., Korea
[3]Electronics and Telecommunications Research Institute, Korea
[1]{wlsxo1119, nlphglee, nlpdrkim}@kangwon.ac.kr
[2]yeonsoo@ncsoft.com
[3]kimyk@etri.re.kr

Abstract

Generative chatbot models based on sequence-to-sequence networks can generate natural conversation interactions if a huge dialogue corpus is used as training data. However, except for a few languages such as English and Chinese, it remains difficult to collect a large dialogue corpus. To address this problem, we propose a chatbot model using a mixture of words and syllables as encoding-decoding units. In addition, we propose a two-step training method, involving pre-training using a large non-dialogue corpus and re-training using a small dialogue corpus. In our experiments, the mixture units were shown to help reduce out-of-vocabulary (OOV) problems. Moreover, the two-step training method was effective in reducing grammatical and semantical errors in responses when the chatbot was trained using a small dialogue corpus (533,997 sentence pairs).

1 Introduction

Chatbots (also known as conversational agents, such as Alexa, Siri, and Cortana) are software programs that mimic written or spoken human speech for interactions with real people. Chatbot models are divided into two types: retrieval-based and generative models. The retrieval-based models match an input query against predefined queries, select one query with the highest matching score, and return a response paired with the selected query. They simply pick responses from a repository of query-response pairs, and therefore the responses do not contain any unplanned grammatical errors. However, the response coverage is restricted, because retrieval-based models cannot handle unseen queries for which predefined responses do not exist. To overcome this problem, generative models have been proposed with the increasing development of deep learning techniques. Generative models do not rely on predefined responses, but rather generate new responses using well-trained neural networks. Therefore, they have an ability to cope effectively with unseen queries. However, they require a large training corpus, in the form of query-response pairs. If the training corpus is not sufficient, then they make grammatical errors, especially in longer sentences.

Many previous studies on generative chatbot models are based on sequence-to-sequence networks called encoder-decoder models (Vinyals and Le, 2015; Shang et al., 2015). To furnish a chatbot with personal characteristics, Li et al. (2016b) proposed a persona-based model in which individual characteristics of speakers are encoded. However, the persona-based model required a large speaker-specific dialogue corpus for model training. To resolve this problem, Luan et al. (2017) proposed a speaker-role adaptation model based on auto-encoding methods using a non-dialogue corpus. To improve the performances of chatbots, Qiu et al. (2017) proposed a hybrid model that generates answers by selecting the most suitable among those retrieved. These previous models require a huge single-turn dialogue corpus (about ten million paired sentences) for training. For most languages, excluding a few such as English and Chinese, it is not easy to collect a high-quality dialogue corpus with millions of entries. To reduce this problem, we propose a two-step training method for efficiently training a generative chatbot model based on a sequence-to-sequence neural network. In the first step, the proposed

Proceedings of the Workshop on Intelligent Interactive Systems and Language Generation (2IS&NLG), pages 31–35,
Tilburg, The Netherlands, November 5 2018.

model is pre-trained using a large amount of non-dialogue text, such as novel texts and news articles. We call this the language learning step. In the second step, it is finaly trained using a comparably small single-turn dialogue corpus. We call this the dialogue learning step. Previous models face difficulties in dealing effectively with out-of-vocabulary (OOV) words. To reduce this problem, we propose an encoding-decoding method using a mixture of words and syllables as encoding-decoding units. The proposed model encodes and decodes closed words (i.e., general nouns and verbs) into word forms. Then, it encodes and decodes open words (i.e., proper nouns and OOV words) into syllable forms.

2 Chatbot Based on Two-Step Training Method and Mixed Encoding-Decoding Units

Figure 1 illustrates the network architecture of the proposed chatbot.

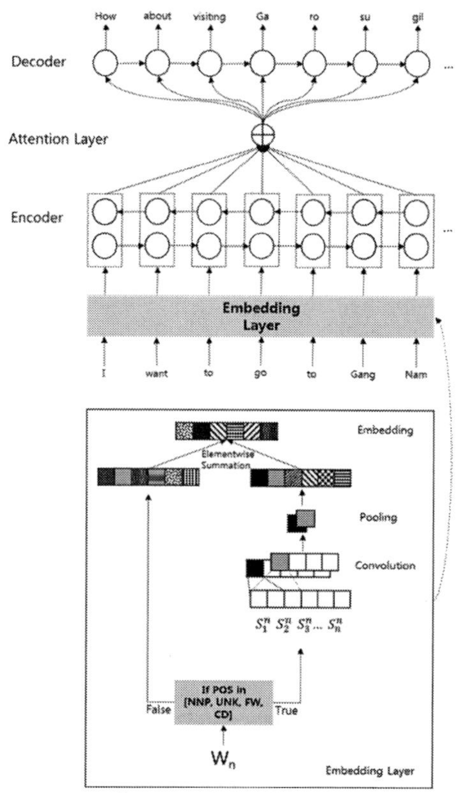

Figure 1: Overall architecture

As shown in Figure 1, the proposed chatbot is based on a sequence-to-sequence network with an attention mechanism (Bahdanau et al., 2015). This differs from conventional sequence-to-sequence networks in the aspect that the encoding and decoding units are not fixed. In the encoder, w_i is the *i*th word embedding vector in an input sentence, and s_k^j is the *j*th syllable embedding vector of the *k*th word in an input sentence. If an input word is included in a closed word category, such as general nouns, verbs, and particles, then the word is input to the sequence-to-sequence network as a word embedding vector. If an input word is not included in a closed word category, but rather in an open word category such as proper nouns or OOV words, then the word is split into syllable sequences, and is merged into an embedding vector using a convolutional neural network (Kim et al., 2016). The merged embedding vector takes the place of an embedding vector for the input word. In the decoder, f_i is the *i*th of the lexical fragments constituting a sentence. The lexical fragment f_i can be a word or syllable. Words in a closed word category are generated in the form of words, and words in an open word category are generated in the form of syllable sequences. To implement this encoding and decoding method, we perform a morphological analysis of the training corpus and split open words into syllable sequences. Then, we use the mixture of words and syllables as an input sequence and output sequence for the sequence-to-sequence network. For example, the single-turn dialogue "A: I want to go to Gangnam. B: How about visiting Garosugil?" is individually split into *[I, want, to, go, to, Gang, nam]* and *[How, about, visiting, Ga, ro, su, gil]*. The former and latter are used as an input and output of the sequence-to-sequence network, respectively.

2.1 Language Learning Step

In the language learning step, we expect that the proposed chatbot learns the grammatical structures of sentences and semantic co-relations between words in a given language. We assume that sentence mimicking can provide some assistance in achieving this goal. To realize this assumption, we adopt an autoencoder mechanism. The proposed chatbot is trained using a large non-dialogue corpus (e.g., news articles) without any turn-taking. During the training, we use each sentence in the non-dialogue corpus as input and output for the sequence-to-sequence network. As a result, the decoder plays the role of a kind of neural language model based on mimicking, which learns how to generate a grammatically and semantically correct sentence. What our model is based on mimicking is a main difference with Ramachandran's model (Ramachandran et al. (2016) based on language modeling (LM).

2.2 Dialogue Learning Step

In the dialogue learning step, we expect that the proposed chatbot learns the degree of association between two sentences in single-turn dialogues. We assume that a chatbot does not require a huge corpus of dialogue examples if it already knows how to generate sentences. To validate this assumption, the dialogue learning step of the proposed chatbot starts after the language learning step is finished. During the training, we employ pairs consisting of a query and response in single-turn dialogue as input and output pairs for the sequence-to-sequence network.

3 Evaluation

3.1 Data Sets and Experimental Settings

For our experiments, we collected two kinds of Korean corpuses: One is a non-dialogue corpus (2,975,918 sentences) consisting of news articles and online forum texts, and the other is a single-turn dialogue corpus (533,997 sentence pairs) collected from mobile chat rooms, in which two users discuss each other's views on a specific topic using the short message service of a commercial telecommunications company. To evaluate the performance of the proposed chatbot, we divided the single-turn dialogue corpus into a dialogue training corpus (499,959 sentence pairs) and a dialogue test corpus (34,038 sentence pairs). We used the whole non-dialogue corpus as training data for the language learning step. Then, we used the dialogue training corpus as training data for the dialogue learning step. The non-dialogue corpus and dialogue training corpus contained 46,334 unique closed words in total. They contained a total of 367,646 unique open words, consisting of 1,120 unique syllables. Therefore, the vocabulary size of the sequence-to-sequence network was set to 47,454 (46,334 unique closed words + 1,120 unique syllables).

We performed an automatic evaluation, as well as a manual evaluation. Automatic evaluation measures for chatbots have been not agreed universally. Portions of word-overlaps between gold-standard answers and chabot's responses are widely used as a practical choice for automatic evaluation. Therefore, we used BLEU (BiLingual Evaluation Understudy) (Papineni et al., 2002) and ROUGE (Recall-Oriented Understudy for Gisting Evaluation) (Lin et al., 2004) as automatic evaluation measures. BLEU was designed to evaluate the quality of text that has been machine-translated from one natural language to another. ROUGE was for designed for evaluating automatic summarization and machine translation software in natural language processing. BLEU and ROUGE were automatically calculated using the test dialogue corpus. It has been reported that these automatic measures may not be suitable for evaluating chatbots (Liu et al. 2016a). Thus, to supplement these evaluation measures, we manually examined outputs of the proposed chatbot from grammatical and semantic viewpoints. For the manual evaluation, we collected 100 new queries from four university students who were not involved in the research. The four students input the queries to the chatbot.–Then, they assigned scores of 0~2 points to each response generated by the chatbot, from both syntactic and semantic viewpoints, as shown in Table 1.

Score	Syntactic Score	Semantic Score
0	A response includes many grammatical errors.	A response is not associated with a query at all.
1	A response includes a few grammatical errors.	A response is partially associated with a query.
2	A response does not include any grammatical errors.	A response is fully associated with a query.

Table 1: Scores for the manual evaluation

3.2 Implementation

We implemented the proposed chatbot using TensorFlow 1.0 (Abadi et al., 2015). Training and prediction were carried out on a per-sentence level. We set the sizes of word embedding vectors and syllable embedding vectors in Figure 1 to 50 and 10, respectively. In the language learning step, the training spanned one epoch, and was performed by mini-batch stochastic gradient descent with a fixed learning rate of 0.001. Each mini-batch consisted of 32 sentences. In the dialogue learning step, the training spanned five epochs, and was performed by mini-batch stochastic gradient descent with a fixed learning rate of 0.001.

Each mini-batch consisted of 32 sentences. During the error backpropagations, the cross-entropy was used as a loss function. The optimal parameters were empirically obtained.

3.3 Experimental Results

The first experiment was designed to show the usefulness of the proposed architecture, where mixtures of words and syllables are used as input and output sequences, from the aspect of OOV problems. Table 2 shows the how the performance of the proposed chatbot varies according to changes in encoding-decoding units.

Measure	Word-Only	Syllable-Only	Mixture
Vocabulary Size	57,102	1,534	55,568
Training Time (h)	2.3	3.2	2.9
BLEU	0.3693 (0.4646)	0.4394 (0.4234)	0.4230 (0.4710)
ROUGE-1	0.2840 (0.3646)	0.4279 (0.4026)	0.3654 (0.4194)
ROUGE-L	0.2657 (0.3861)	0.4177 (0.3920)	0.3518 (0.4009)
Syntactic Score	0.43	0.98	0.70
Semantic Score	0.62	1.26	0.98

Table 2: Performance comparison according to different encoding and decoding units

In Table 2, *Mixture* is the proposed model. *Word-Only* and *Syllable-Only* represent chatbots that use only words and syllables, respectively, as encoding-decoding units. The parenthesized scores are the performances when functional words (i.e., ending words, postpositional words, and so on) in Korean are excluded from the performance evaluations. In other words, they are the performances with respect to generated content words (i.e., nouns, verbs, and so on). All of the models were trained using only the dialogue training corpus, like conventional chatbot models. As shown in Table 2, *Mixture* exhibited a better performance than *Word-Only* for all measures. Although *Mixture* achieved an inferior performance to *Syllable-Only* for the measures with respect to all types of words, it outperformed *Syllable-Only* for the measures with respect to just content words. We found that *Word-Only* and *Syllable-Only* made many mistakes in generating content words that were unseen in the training data. This fact indirectly shows that the proposed architecture may contribute to reducing OOV problems. We analyzed the cases in which *Mixture* showed lower syntactic and semantic scores than *Syllable-Only*. The reasons are as follows: *Syllable-Only* showed relatively high syntactic and semantic scores because it often returns short and general responses like "Okay" and "Yes, I see". Moreover, *Syllable-Only* more correctly generated functional words than *Word-Only* and *Mixture* did. As a result, *Syllable-Only* obtained higher syntactic and semantic scores. Although *Mixture* well generated content words, it showed lower syntactic and semantic scores than *Syllable-Only* because it less correctly generated functional words.

The second experiment was designed to show the effectiveness of the proposed training method. Table 3 shows how the performance of the proposed chatbot varies according to different training methods. In Table 3, *Single-Step Training* is a conventional training method in which a chatbot is trained using only the dialogue training corpus. *LM Training* is the training method proposed by Ramachandran et al. (2016). In LM Training, a chatbot is pre-trained using a language model, and re-trained using the dialogue training corpus. *Two-Step Training* is the proposed method, in which the chatbot is pre-trained using the non-dialogue corpus and re-trained using the dialogue training corpus. The parenthesized scores give the performances when functional words are excluded from the performance evaluations.

Measure	Single-Step Training	LM Training	Two-Step Training
BLEU	0.4230 (0.4710)	0.4592 (0.5094)	0.4591 (0.5076)
ROUGE-1	0.3654 (0.4194)	0.3833 (0.4231)	0.4045 (0.4673)
ROUGE-L	0.3518 (0.4009)	0.3858 (0.4379)	0.4004 (0.4666)
Syn. Score	0.70	0.81	0.94
Sem. Score	0.98	1.09	1.30

Table 3: Performance comparison according to different training methods

As shown in Table 3, *Two-Step Training* outperformed *Single-Step Training* for most measures and showed competitive performances compared with *LM Training* for the ROUGE scores of content words. In particular, *Two-Step Training* achieved much higher scores than *Single-Step Training* and *LM Training* in the manual evaluation. This fact reveals that the proposed training method can be effective in reducing grammatical errors of responses and in generating responses associated with input queries when a dialogue corpus is not sufficient to train chatbots based on sequence-to-sequence networks.

4 Conclusion

We have proposed a chatbot model using a modified architecture of a sequence-to-sequence network. The chatbot used a mixture of words and syllables as encoding-decoding units, in order to reduce OOV problems. In addition, we proposed a new training method to pre-train the chatbot using a large non-dialogue corpus, and to re-train the chatbot using a small dialogue corpus. This training method contributed to reducing syntactic and semantic mistakes when a dialogue corpus for training is not large enough.

Acknowledgments

This work was supported by 2017 research grant funded by NCSOFT corp. and Institute for Information & communications Technology Promotion (IITP) grant funded by the Korea government (MSIT) (R0126-15-1117, Core technology development of the spontaneous speech dialogue processing for the language learning). In addition, this work was partly supported by the National Research Foundation of Korea Grant funded by the Korean Government (NRF-2017M3C4A7068188).

References

Vinyals, O., & Le, Q. (2015). A neural conversational model. *arXiv preprint arXiv:1506.05869*.

Shang, L., Lu, Z., & Li, H. (2015). Neural responding machine for short-text conversation. *arXiv preprint arXiv:1503.02364*.

Li, J., Galley, M., Brockett, C., Spithourakis, G. P., Gao, J., & Dolan, B. (2016). A persona-based neural conversation model. *arXiv preprint arXiv:1603.06155*.

Luan, Y., Brockett, C., Dolan, B., Gao, J., & Galley, M. (2017). Multi-Task Learning for Speaker-Role Adaptation in Neural Conversation Models. *arXiv preprint arXiv:1710.07388*.

Qiu, M., Li, F. L., Wang, S., Gao, X., Chen, Y., Zhao, W., ... & Chu, W. (2017). Alime chat: A sequence to sequence and rerank based chatbot engine. In *Proceedings of the 55th Annual Meeting of the Association for Computational Linguistics (Volume 2: Short Papers)* (Vol. 2, pp. 498-503).

Kim, Y., Jernite, Y., Sontag, D., & Rush, A. M. (2016, February). Character-Aware Neural Language Models. In *AAAI* (pp. 2741-2749).

Bahdanau, D., Cho, K., & Bengio, Y. (2014). Neural machine translation by jointly learning to align and translate. *arXiv preprint arXiv:1409.0473*.

Papineni, K., Roukos, S., Ward, T., & Zhu, W. J. (2002, July). BLEU: a method for automatic evaluation of machine translation. In *Proceedings of the 40th annual meeting on association for computational linguistics* (pp. 311-318). Association for Computational Linguistics.

Lin, C. Y. (2004). Rouge: A package for automatic evaluation of summaries. *Text Summarization Branches Out*.

Liu, C. W., Lowe, R., Serban, I. V., Noseworthy, M., Charlin, L., & Pineau, J. (2016). How not to evaluate your dialogue system: An empirical study of unsupervised evaluation metrics for dialogue response generation. *arXiv preprint arXiv:1603.08023*.

M. Abadi, A. Agarwal, P. Barham, E. Brevdo, Z. Chen, C. Citro, G. S. Corrado, A. Davis, J. Dean, M. Devin, S. Ghemawat, I. Goodfellow, A. Harp, G. Irving, M. Isard, Y. Jia, R. Jozefowicz, L. Kaiser, M. Kudlur, J. Levenberg, D. Mane,´ R. Monga, S. Moore, D. Murray, C. Olah, M. Schuster, J. Shlens, B. Steiner, I. Sutskever, K. Talwar, P. Tucker, V. Vanhoucke, V. Vasudevan, F. Viegas, O. Vinyals, P. War- ´ den, M. Wattenberg, M. Wicke, Y. Yu, and X. Zheng. (2016, November). TensorFlow: A System for Large-Scale Machine Learning. In *OSDI* (Vol. 16, pp. 265-283).

Ramachandran, P., Liu, P. J., & Le, Q. V. (2016). Unsupervised pretraining for sequence to sequence learning. *arXiv preprint arXiv:1611.02683*.

Supporting Content Design with an Eye Tracker: The Case of Weather-based Recommendations

Alejandro Catala, Jose M. Alonso, and Alberto Bugarin

Centro Singular de Investigación en Tecnoloxías da Información (CiTIUS),
Universidade de Santiago de Compostela, Spain
{alejandro.catala, josemaria.alonso.moral, alberto.bugarin.diz}@usc.es

Abstract

Designing content output for weather-aware services based on domain experts can sometimes be arduous due to their limited availability and the amount and complexity of information considered in explaining their recommendations. As an initial step in our work towards generating recommendations that are acceptable and readable, our methodology involving an eye tracker attempts to simplify and capture more valuable data in early design stages. Our pilot study explored which information in weather-based recommendations seemed to be more useful to support users decision making. The results suggest that interactive content could be deployed based on the relevance of informational items and both graphical points of interest and legends could help in delivering content more efficiently.

1 Introduction

In the realm of context-aware services and interactive applications, Natural Language Generation (NLG) involving maps in combination with meteorological data is subject to active field research (Ramos-Soto et al., 2015). Automatically generating recommendations consisting of both text and figures can help users in making decisions while providing personalized services (Gkatzia et al., 2017). Furthermore, it is not just an issue of giving a suitable recommendation according to the user's context (Mocholi et al., 2012), but also to design content generators in such a way that the artificial intelligence associated to the service is better considered in terms of being explainable, accountable and intelligible (Abdul et al., 2018; Alonso et al., 2018).

The combination of such qualities means that we are facing a complex design problem that needs to deal with several issues before a successful algorithm can be implemented. In order to start addressing this issue, we propose to use an eye tracker with a double purpose: i) to set a priority and get a narrower focus on all the information elicited from meteorologists; and ii) to supply a method in order to gather from users more objective data that complement self-reporting questionnaires. In this way, we expect to enable better informed design decisions. Thus, this paper contributes a pilot empirical study exploring with the help of an eye tracker how stimuli containing recommendations with explanations supported by figures are processed by people and which elements can be more relevant for generating content in future designs.

2 Background on cognitive psychology and eye tracking

Eye trackers are devices capable of recording gaze or eye-movement data as users focus their visual attention. They have typically supported research concerned about reading patterns and content engagement (Liu, 2014), since visual attention triggers underlying cognitive processes. There are also studies regarding how the required tasks can influence people's eye movements (Kaakinen and Hyona, 2010). In addition, it is well-known from cognitive psychology that multimodal texts and underlying structures can enhance interaction with contents and their processing effort (Danielsson and Selander, 2016). For example, the study in (Holsanova et al., 2008) used an eye tracker to confirm that design principles such as spatial contiguity and attentional guidance that support both spatial navigation and semantic integration of concepts facilitate information processing in newspa-

Proceedings of the Workshop on Intelligent Interactive Systems and Language Generation (2IS&NLG), pages 36–41,
Tilburg, The Netherlands, November 5 2018.

per reading.

In order to analyze gaze data, there are several features and a range of metrics that eye-tracking tools can provide, as surveyed in (Sharafi et al., 2015). Among the raw data, eye fixations are especially useful, which refer to stabilization of the eye for a period of time (e.g. circa 200ms) and provide deeper understanding on where visual attention has been focused. Scanpaths are also interesting, which visualize chains of fixations. To the best of our knowledge, there is not much specific work using eye-tracking to explore weather-based stimuli besides the recent study by (Sivle and Uppstad, 2018). The authors explored how multimodal reading takes place and why readers move between representations, concluding that tables are more often used with respect to diagrams.

3 Study

3.1 Participants and equipment

Fifteen adult volunteers (mean: 23.13 years old, sd=2.71) participated in the empirical study. They were all postgraduate students or PhD candidates working on technical fields related to computer science. All except one stated to have prior knowledge of Galician geography.

The experimental setting was implemented using the EyeTribe Tracker[1] to track the eye gaze on a main screen where the stimuli were displayed (see Figure 1). Also, a device supported the subject's chin to prevent tracker calibration issues. A secondary bigger screen only active while answering questionnaires was set behind, placed at a distance so that both can be read without changing the pose, to not compromise the tracker calibration.

We used the Ogama software (Voßkühler et al., 2008) (version 5.0.5754) to assemble the stimuli and manage the gaze data recording.

3.2 Stimuli design

The empirical study consisted of 6 trials, which were randomized to prevent order effects. The stimulus in each trial included a recommendation about the suitability to carry out activities on the Beach, Surfing or activities on the Mountains. Typically, a stimulus included a textual description on the upper side of the screen. The text was in Spanish, the native language of the participants. A literal transcription of a sample text on the Beach topic into English is as follows:

[1] https://github.com/EyeTribe/documentation

Figure 1: Experimental setting.

"Today will be a perfect day to enjoy the beaches of A Mariña luguesa, like in As Catedrais or Arealonga, since the temperatures will be very pleasant and the skies will remain clear all day. Likewise, it is also recommended to attend the fluvial beaches of the interior of Galicia.
The reason for the good weather prevailing on the Cantabrian coast and inland of Galicia is due to the move of the Anticyclone from the Azores to the east. Such a synoptic situation will cause both territories to be left out of the mists and low cloud cover that will do affect the Galician Atlantic coast."

The text consisted of both a recommendation *R* (the first paragraph) and an explanation of the weather forecast *E* (the second paragraph). The order of these parts can lead to two possible arrangements (i.e., <*R*, *E*> or <*E*, *R*>). The stimuli also came with a set of maps supporting the explanation (see Figure 2-Left): weather forecast, UV index, max temperature, and sea state maps. The fourth map was replaced by a storm warning map in the mountain recommendations. The stimuli were designed by a meteorologist with experience in generating weather reports, taking into account that the target user is the general public.

3.3 Procedure

Before the experimental session, each participant was provided with an informed consent form explaining the research context and empirical tasks, and agreed to participate voluntarily. Then, the experimenter proceeded to make the adjustments to the chair as needed, and a calibration procedure was carried out in order to initialize the eye tracker and ensure gaze data recording. Some informational screens were displayed regarding geographical information to get acquainted with the type of maps and related locations. Then the user performed the trials following instructions on the main screen, just switching to the secondary display when requested to answer questionnaires. For each trial, there was a first screen presenting the textual description as a stimulus. The task was to read the text, in order to gather typical reading patterns, warm up, and be sure that tracking worked correctly. A second screen presented the same text plus the figures supporting the textual description. The task for the user was to inspect the recommendation to assess to which extent the visual information provided matched the textual description. The stimuli were self-paced, and participants kept their hand on the space bar all the time, which had to be pushed to move forward. Switching between displays was handled by the experimenter, turning them off and on as needed. Instruction screens were set between stimuli in order to ensure that gaze recording was separated accordingly. Once the 6 trials were finished, the participant answered the demographics questionnaire.

3.4 Results

3.4.1 Gaze data

We carried out a qualitative analysis by replaying the fixations, scanpaths and calculating the attention maps as fixation count heatmaps with fixations weighted by duration as provided by the Ogama software. While fixations just give point clouds where users looked at on screen, the attention maps can be used to identify regions of special attention in specific stimuli, filtering noise and enhancing visual analysis. Longer fixations, and therefore attention, have several implications. In reading tasks, longer fixations are typically over words that took longer processing time (Rauzy and Blache, 2012; Sharafi et al., 2015), either because the word was more difficult to understand or just because it was considered a relevant and important term to remember. In matching tasks, fixations and attention maps provide insight into which spots can be more informational and relevant to support the textual description. This allows us to decide which information should be kept as it is, highlighted or discarded.

In the reading tasks, we captured the reading patterns, which led to scanpaths line per line from left to right. It took on average about 29 seconds (sd=7.99), resulting in 91.28 (sd=22.97) fixations and 3.18 fixations per second on average. The attention maps show that more processing effort focused on the general forecast description E rather than in the recommendation R itself regardless of the arrangement. We must also be aware that explanations were usually longer than the proper recommendation. When analyzing the words lying in the spots, the most prominent ones are related to weather events (e.g., showers, wind, or very significant waves) and geographical locations (e.g., Patos beach, A Madalena beach, or province of Pontevedra). Also, we noticed that some single words (e.g., *synoptic*) were signaled, which are uncommon terms often used by meteorologists.

In the matching tasks, each trial took 24.42 seconds on average (sd=9.71), with a mean number of fixations about 70.28 (sd=26.67) and 2.9 fixations per second. Regarding the gaze data, weather events and geographical locations are again prominent in the text (e.g., light showers, high temperature, inland region, or beach of Carnota). Regarding the figures, the most prominent spots are over the weather forecast map (e.g., related to specific areas mentioned in the text such as *A Mariña luguesa* in Figure 2-Center), the max temperature map and the maps' legends. When the gaze focused longer on weather graphic symbols, they were about weather events such as showers rather than good weather conditions. The sea and the storm warning maps had some relevant role in the surfing and mountain trials respectively as depicted in Figure 2-Right. Overall, the dwell times on the defined Areas of Interests (AOIs) confirm the relevance of maps for users (see Figure 3).

3.4.2 Questionnaires

We gathered additional information through questionnaires provided after each trial. We used a 7-point Likert scale for assessing questions regarding *Coherence text-graphics* (m=6.26, sd=1.13), *Readability* (m=6.23, sd=1.02), and *Understandability* (m=6.37, sd=0.98). Some open questions to gather the most and less relevant items according to participants were included. Table 1 reports the frequencies of topics in the content analysis. Overall, these self-reported remarks were consistent with the observation from the gaze data.

4 Discussion and future work

We have explored eye-tracking as a complementary method to the self-reporting questionnaires that are typically used in similar research.

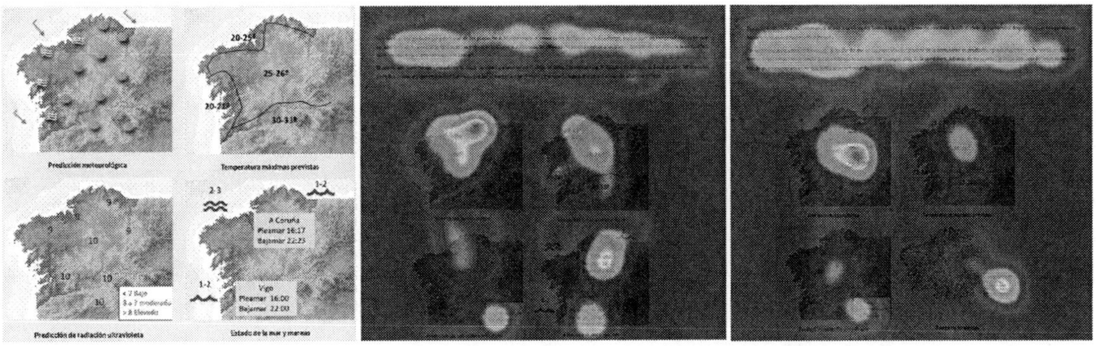

Figure 2: Sample maps (Left). Attention maps for a beach (Center) and a mountain stimulus (Right), calculated as fixation count height maps with fixations weighted by duration and using the following colour scale normalization: purple (10%), blue (25%), turquoise (40%), green (65%), yellow (75%), orange (93%), red (100%). The stimuli size was 1920x1080, the kernel size was Ogama's default 201.

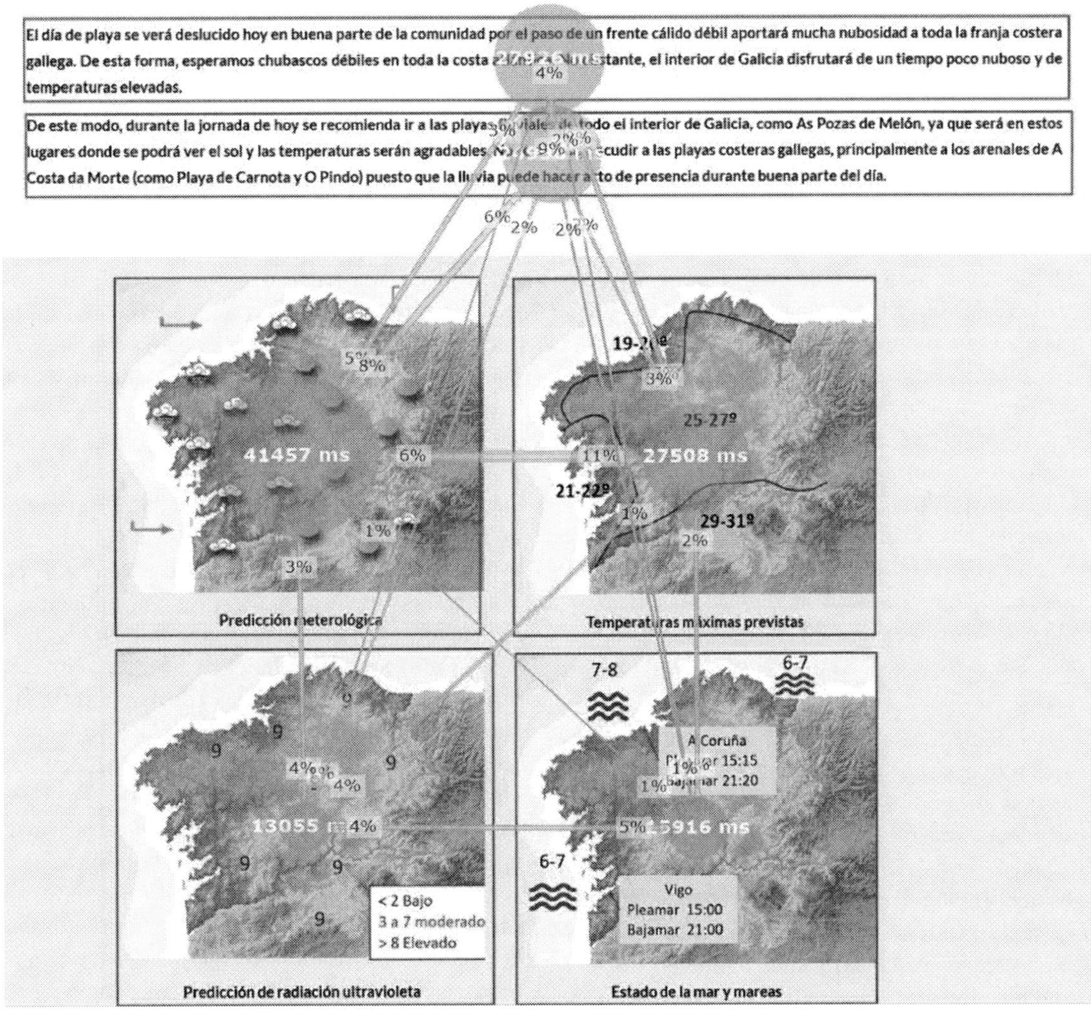

Figure 3: Complete fixation time on Areas of Interests (AOIs) and relative transition paths for a Beach stimulus. It provides a magnitude for the overall time spent in each AOI.

Table 1: Content analysis: the most '+' and less '-' relevant items (number of occurrences in brackets).

	Beach	Surfing	Mountain
+	weather forecast map (7), max temperature map (4), UV index map (2), sea state map (2)	sea state map (7)	weather forecast map (8), storm warning map (4), max temperature map (3)
-	complex descriptions including either technical terms or place names (5), UV index (3)	max temperature map (2), UV index map (2), place names (3)	place names and technical terms, storm warning map if there is no risk

Involving domain experts to provide well-founded descriptions and explanations is a challenge. They provide much information to be fully precise, and therefore prioritizing or simplifying the pieces of information is not straightforward.

Following a traditional approach would require several design cycles to elicit information from meteorologists, who are not always available, whereas testing with users is costly even for small samples. Thus, our approach attempts to speed up the process at an early stage of development by starting with a more exploratory scenario that allowed us to get multiple observations at once in order to back up future design decisions. This motivated that our request to the meteorologist for designing the stimuli included some practical constraints such as text no longer than a short paragraph and no more than four maps fitting a single screen for a web service application. In this way, the expert still had some room to create a report and we are not discarding informational items beforehand without a good reason. Moreover, having a setting with a PC desktop screen was deliberately chosen because we can focus on the content without any interference imposed by interactions (e.g., navigating between smaller screens in a mobile user interface), and the design space is better understood by both the domain expert and users.

The results confirmed that the domain expert who designed the stimuli used more source information than users demand and can naturally process, as suggested by underused maps and user comments regarding complex descriptions and technical terms. Thus, one design principle is to provide *simplified on-screen information*. Choosing a limited set of information sources would help to reduce complexity and cognitive load. For example, by providing only the two most relevant maps as reported in the results and by giving the option to interactively explore more complex and extended information. Salient gaze spots for text were on referring expressions, such as proper nouns of places, and weather events. This is an expected result as these words are actually the key information being conveyed, in line with (Rauzy and Blache, 2012).

When talking about specific places (e.g., the name of a beach or a peak), the maps should also include landmarks to facilitate its interpretation, mitigate any gap in the user's geographical background knowledge and simplify text. Furthermore, when text is the only possible output, because maps are not available or another modality is being used (e.g., speech), the *specific place should be accompanied of a more general location*. For example, a recommendation referring to the beach called "Patos" could be improved by expanding the information in the text with a more general location well-known by users such as *Ría de Vigo*. We can also focus on the recommendation *R*, and then consider the general *explanation in a follow-up interaction*. This is still important to provide more intelligibly context-aware applications (Lim and Dey, 2013). Expanded explanations under request could include a more technical view indeed. We must *use the legends properly* as can be a very powerful resource, with users looking at them systematically. Although using heatmaps can be a very useful tool, they must be handled with care to prevent misinterpretations (Bojko, 2009). Our study used fixation count height maps with a correction to take into account the length of fixations. However, we must be aware that they just represent average fixation behaviour, and as any averaged computation it can be subject to bias due to very different fixation behaviours or longer exposures to the stimuli. Accordingly, more advance and robust computations to complement and counteract such limitations should be considered whenever possible.

We can conclude that an eye-tracker provides additional objective and valuable data which are complementary, but quite in agreement to those derived from questionnaires. As future work, we aim to develop a data-to-text module ready to automatically produce multimodal recommendations. Content design will be initially guided by the conclusions derived from this study. Furthermore, we will analyze how other different structures (that can be explored interactively) may affect the explainability and intelligibility of a weather-aware service.

Acknowledgements

This work has been partially funded by the Spanish Ministry of Economy and Competitiveness under the project grants BAI4SOW (TIN2014-56633-C3-1-R), BIGBISC (TIN2017-84796-C2-1-R), and the Ramón y Cajal Research grant RYC-2016-19802, by the European Regional Development Fund (ERDF/FEDER program) and Consellería de Cultura, Educación e Ordenación Universitaria (acc.2016-2019, ED431G/08), and by the CiTIUS Summer scholarship program. Special thanks go to Damian Caballero for his invaluable help and expertise on weather recommendations and forecasting. Thanks to all volunteers who participated in the study.

References

Ashraf Abdul, Jo Vermeulen, Danding Wang, Brian Y. Lim, and Mohan Kankanhalli. 2018. Trends and trajectories for explainable, accountable and intelligible systems: An hci research agenda. In *Proceedings of the 2018 CHI Conference on Human Factors in Computing Systems*, CHI '18, pages 582:1–582:18, New York, NY, USA. ACM.

Jose M. Alonso, C. Castiello, and C. Mencar. 2018. A bibliometric analysis of the explainable artificial intelligence research field. In *17th International Conference on Information Processing and Management of Uncertainty in Knowledge-Based Systems*, pages 3–15. Springer.

Agnieszka (Aga) Bojko. 2009. Informative or misleading? heatmaps deconstructed. In *Human-Computer Interaction. New Trends*, pages 30–39, Berlin, Heidelberg. Springer Berlin Heidelberg.

Kristina Danielsson and Staffan Selander. 2016. Reading multimodal texts for learning : a model for cultivating multimodal literacy. *Designs for Learning*, 8(1):25–36.

Dimitra Gkatzia, Oliver Lemon, and Verena Rieser. 2017. Data-to-text generation improves decision-making under uncertainty. *IEEE Computational Intelligence Magazine*, 12(3):10–17.

Jana Holsanova, Nils Holmberg, and Kenneth Holmqvist. 2008. Reading information graphics: The role of spatial contiguity and dual attentional guidance. *Applied Cognitive Psychology*, 23(9):1215–1226.

Johanna K. Kaakinen and Jukka Hyona. 2010. Task effects on eye movements during reading. *Journal of Experimental Psychology: Learning, Memory, and Cognition*, 36(6):1561–1566.

Brian Y. Lim and Anind K. Dey. 2013. Evaluating intelligibility usage and usefulness in a context-aware application. In *Human-Computer Interaction. Towards Intelligent and Implicit Interaction*, pages 92–101, Berlin, Heidelberg. Springer Berlin Heidelberg.

Pei-Lin Liu. 2014. Using eye tracking to understand learners' reading process through the concept-mapping learning strategy. *Computers & Education*, 78:237 – 249.

Jose A. Mocholi, Javier Jaen, Kamil Krynicki, Alejandro Catala, Artzai Picón, and Alejandro Cadenas. 2012. Learning semantically-annotated routes for context-aware recommendations on map navigation systems. *Applied Soft Computing*, 12(9):3088 – 3098.

Alejandro Ramos-Soto, Alberto Jose Bugarín, Senen Barro, and Juan Taboada. 2015. Linguistic descriptions for automatic generation of textual short-term weather forecasts on real prediction data. *IEEE Transactions on Fuzzy Systems*, 23(1):44–57.

Stéphane Rauzy and Philippe Blache. 2012. Robustness and processing difficulty models. A pilot study for eye-tracking data on the French Treebank. In *Workshop on Eye-tracking and Natural Language Processing at The 24th International Conference on Computational Linguistics (COLING)*, Proceedings of the First Workshop on Eye-tracking and Natural Language Processing, pages 1–15, Mumbai, India.

Zohreh Sharafi, Timothy Shaffer, Bonita Sharif, and Yann-Gaël Guéhéneuc. 2015. Eye-tracking metrics in software engineering. In *2015 Asia-Pacific Software Engineering Conference (APSEC)*, pages 96–103.

Anders D Sivle and Per H Uppstad. 2018. Reasons for relating representations when reading digital multimodal science information. *Visual Communication*, 17(3):313–336.

Adrian Voßkühler, Volkhard Nordmeier, Lars Kuchinke, and Arthur M. Jacobs. 2008. Ogama (open gaze and mouse analyzer): Open-source software designed to analyze eye and mouse movements in slideshow study designs. *Behavior Research Methods*, 40(4):1150–1162.

ChatEval: A Tool for the Systematic Evaluation of Chatbots

João Sedoc* **Daphne Ippolito*** **Arun Kirubarajan** **Jai Thirani** **Lyle Ungar** **Chris Callison-Burch**
*Authors contributed equally
University of Pennsylvania
{joao,daphnei,kiruba,jthirani,ungar,ccb}@seas.upenn.edu

Abstract

Open-domain dialog systems are difficult to evaluate. The current best practice for analyzing and comparing these dialog systems is the use of human judgments. However, the lack of standardization in evaluation procedures, and the fact that model parameters and code are rarely published hinder systematic human evaluation experiments. We introduce a unified framework for human evaluation of chatbots that augments existing chatbot tools, and provides a web-based hub for researchers to share and compare their dialog systems. Researchers can submit their trained models to the ChatEval web interface and obtain comparisons with baselines and prior work. The evaluation code is open-source to ensure evaluation is performed in a standardized and transparent way. In addition, we introduce open-source baseline models and evaluation datasets. ChatEval can be found at `https://chateval.org`.

Introduction

Reproducibility and model assessment for open-domain dialog systems is challenging, as many small variations in the training setup or evaluation technique can result in large differences in perceived model performance. In addition, as the field has grown, it has become increasingly fragmented.

Papers often focus on novel methods, but insufficient attention has been paid to ensuring that datasets and evaluation remain consistent and reproducible. For example, while human evaluation of chatbot quality is extremely common, few papers publish the set of prompts used for this evaluation, and almost no papers release their learned model parameters. Because of this, papers tend to evaluate their methodological improvement against a sequence-to-sequence (Seq2Seq) baseline (Sutskever et al., 2014) rather than against each other.

Seq2Seq was first proposed for dialog generation by Vinyals and Le (2015) in a system they called the Neural Conversational Model (NCM). Due to the NCM being closed-source, nearly all the papers comparing against it have implemented their own versions, with widely varying performance. Indeed, we found no model, neither among those we trained nor those available online, that matched the performance of the original NCM, as evaluated by humans.

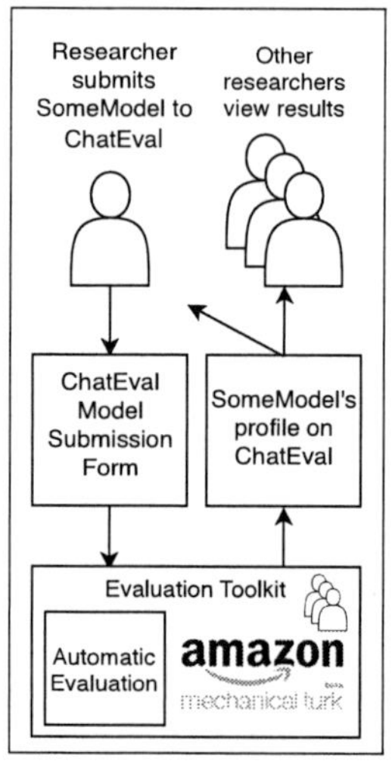

Figure 1: Flow of information in ChatEval. A researcher submits information about her model, including its responses to prompts in a standard evaluation set. Automatic evaluation as well as human evaluation are conducted, then the results are posted publicly on the ChatEval website.

Another issue is that human evaluation experiments, which are currently the gold standard for model evaluation, are equally fragmented, with almost no two papers by different authors adopting the same evaluation dataset or experimental procedure.

To address these concerns, we have built ChatEval, a scientific framework for evaluating chatbots. ChatEval consists of two main components: (1) an open-source codebase for conducting automatic and human evaluation of chatbots in a standardized way, and (2) a web portal for accessing model code, trained parameters, and evaluation results, which grows with participation. In addition, ChatEval includes newly created and cu-

Proceedings of the Workshop on Intelligent Interactive Systems and Language Generation (2IS&NLG), pages 42–44,
Tilburg, The Netherlands, November 5 2018.

rated evaluation datasets with both human annotated and automated baselines.

Related Work

Competitions such as the Alexa Prize,[1], ConvAI[2] and WOCHAT,[3] rank submitted chatbots by having humans converse with them and then rate the quality of the conversation. However, asking for absolute assessments of quality yields less discriminative results than soliciting direct comparisons of quality. In the dataset introduced for the ConvAI2 competition, nearly all the proposed algorithms were evaluated to be within one standard deviation of each other (Zhang et al., 2018). Therefore, for our human evaluation task, we ask humans to directly compare the responses of two models given the previous utterances in the conversation.

Both Facebook and Amazon have developed evaluation systems that allow humans to converse with (and then rate) a chatbot (Venkatesh et al., 2018; Miller et al., 2017). Facebook's ParlAI [4] is the most comparable system for a unified framework for sharing, training, and evaluating chatbots; however, ChatEval is different in that it entirely focuses on the evaluation and warehousing of models. Our infrastructure relies only on output text files, and does not require any code base integration .

The ChatEval Web Interface

The ChatEval web interface consists of four primary pages. Aside from the overview page, there is a model submission form, a page for viewing the profile of any submitted model, and a page for comparing the responses of multiple models.

Model Submission When researchers submit their model for evaluation, they are also asked to submit the following: A description of model which could include link to paper or project page. The model's responses on at least one of our evaluation datasets. Researcher may also optionally submit a URL to a public code repository and a URL to download trained model parameters.

After the code and model parameters are manually checked, we use the ChatEval evaluation toolkit to launch evaluation on the submitted responses. Two-choice human evaluation experiments compare the researchers' model against baselines of their choice. New models submitted to the ChatEval system become available for future researchers to compare against. Automatic evaluation metrics are also computed. At the researchers' request, results may be embargoed prior to publication.

Model Profile Each submitted model as well as each of our baseline models have a profile page on the ChatEval website. The profile consists of the URLs and description provided by the researcher, the responses of the model to each prompt in the evaluation set, and a visualization of the results of human and automatic evaluation.

Response Comparison To facilitate qualitative comparison of models, we offer a response comparison interface where users can see all the prompts in a particular evaluation set, and the responses generated by each model.

Evaluation Toolkit

The ChatEval evaluation toolkit is used to evaluate submitted models. It consists of an automatic evaluation and a human evaluation component.

Automatic Evaluation Automatic evaluation metrics include: The number of unique n-grams in the model's responses divided by the total number of generated tokens. Average cosine-similarity between the mean of the word embeddings of a generated response and ground-truth response (Liu et al., 2016). Sentence average BLEU-2 score (Liu et al., 2016). Response perplexity, measured using the likelihood that the model predicts the correct. response (Zhang et al., 2018). Our system is easily extensible to support other evaluation metrics.

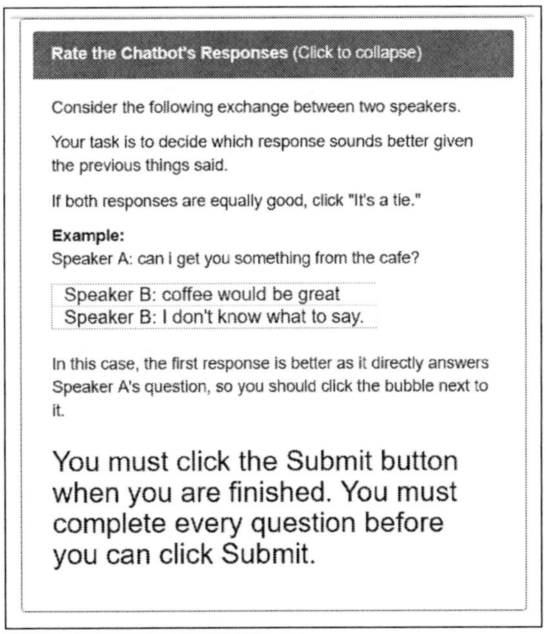

Figure 2: The instructions seen by AMT workers.

Human Evaluation A/B comparison tests consist of showing the evaluator a prompt and two possible responses from models which are being compared. The

[1]https://developer.amazon.com/alexaprize
[2]http://convai.io/
[3]http://workshop.colips.org/wochat/
[4]https://parl.ai

prompt can consist of a single utterance or a series of utterances. The user picks the better response or specifies a tie. When both responses are the same, a tie is automatically recorded. The instructions seen by AMT workers are shown in Figure 2.

The evaluation prompts are split into blocks (currently defaulted to 10). Crowd workers are paid $0.01 per single evaluation. We used three evaluators per prompt, so, if there are 200 prompt/response pairs, we have 600 ratings and the net cost of the experiment is $6. On the submission form, we ask researchers to pay for the cost of the AMT experiment.

The overall inter-annotator agreement (IAA) varies depending on the vagueness of the prompt as well as the similarity of the models. Out of 18 different experiments run, we found that IAA, as measured by Cohen's weighted kappa (Cohen, 1968), varies between .2 to .54 if we include tie choices. This is similar to the findings of Yuwono et al. who also found low inter-annotator agreement. Unfortunately, there are occasionally bad workers, which we automatically remove from our results. In order to identify such workers, we examine the worker against the other annotators.

Evaluation Datasets

We propose using the dataset collected by the dialogue breakdown detection (DBDC) task (Higashinaka et al., 2017) as a standard benchmark. The DBDC dataset was created by presenting participants with a short paragraph of context and then asking them to converse with three possible chatbots: TikTok, Iris, and CIC. Participants knew that they were speaking with a chatbot, and the conversations reflect this. We randomly selected 200 human utterances from this dataset, after manually filtering out utterances which were too ambiguous or short to be easily answerable. As the DBDC dataset does not contain any human-human dialog, we collected reference human responses to each utterance.

For compatibility with prior work, we also publish random subsets of 200 query-response pairs from the test sets of Twitter and OpenSubtitles. We also make available the list of 200 prompts used as the evaluation set by Vinyals and Le (2015) in their analysis of the NCM's performance.

The datasets used for chatbot evaluation ought to reflect the goal of the chatbot. For example, even if a chatbot is trained on Twitter, it only makes sense to evaluate on Twitter if the chatbot's aim is to be skilled at responding to Tweets. With the DBDC dataset, we emphasize the goal of engaging in text-based interactions with users who know they are speaking with a chatbot. We believe that this dataset best represents the kind of conversations we would expect a user to actually have with a text-based conversational agent.

Conclusion

ChatEval is a framework for systematic evaluation of chatbots. Specifically, it is a repository of model code and parameters, evaluation sets, model comparisons, and a standard human evaluation setup. ChatEval seemlessly allows researchers to make systematic and consistent comparisons of conversational agents. We hope that future researchers–and the entire field–will benefit from ChatEval.

References

Jacob Cohen. 1968. Weighted kappa: Nominal scale agreement provision for scaled disagreement or partial credit. *Psychological bulletin*, 70(4):213.

Ryuichiro Higashinaka, Kotaro Funakoshi, Michimasa Inaba, Yuiko Tsunomori, Tetsuro Takahashi, and Nobuhiro Kaji. 2017. Overview of dialogue breakdown detection challenge 3. *Proceedings of Dialog System Technology Challenge*, 6.

Chia-Wei Liu, Ryan Lowe, Iulian Serban, Mike Noseworthy, Laurent Charlin, and Joelle Pineau. 2016. How not to evaluate your dialogue system: An empirical study of unsupervised evaluation metrics for dialogue response generation. In *EMNLP*, pages 2122–2132. Association for Computational Linguistics.

Alexander Miller, Will Feng, Dhruv Batra, Antoine Bordes, Adam Fisch, Jiasen Lu, Devi Parikh, and Jason Weston. 2017. Parlai: A dialog research software platform. In *EMNLP*, pages 79–84. Association for Computational Linguistics.

Ilya Sutskever, Oriol Vinyals, and Quoc V Le. 2014. Sequence to sequence learning with neural networks. In *NIPS*, pages 3104–3112.

Anu Venkatesh, Chandra Khatri, Ashwin Ram, Fenfei Guo, Raefer Gabriel, Ashish Nagar, Rohit Prasad, Ming Cheng, Behnam Hedayatnia, Angeliki Metallinou, Rahul Goel, Shaohua Yang, and Anirudh Raju. 2018. On Evaluating and Comparing Conversational Agents. (Nips):1–10.

Oriol Vinyals and Quoc V. Le. 2015. A Neural Conversational Model. *Natural Language Dialog Systems and Intelligent Assistants*, 37:233–239.

Steven Kester Yuwono, Wu Biao, and Luis Fernando DHaro. Automated scoring of chatbot responses in conversational dialogue.

Saizheng Zhang, Emily Dinan, Jack Urbanek, Arthur Szlam, Douwe Kiela, and Jason Weston. 2018. Personalizing Dialogue Agents: I have a dog, do you have pets too? pages 1–14.

CheckYourMeal!: diet management with NLG

Luca Anselma, **Simone Donetti**, **Alessandro Mazzei**, and **Andrea Pirone**

[anselma,donetti,mazzei,pirone]@di.unito.it
Dipartimento di Informatica
Università degli Studi di Torino
C.so Svizzera 185, 10149 Torino, Italy

Abstract

CheckYourMeal! is an app designed to manage the diet of a user. The app is a component of a complex cloud architecture designed for assisting users in their interaction with food during a week. CheckYourMeal! allows to show the results of automatic reasoning in both graphical and textual forms. In particular, the bilingual English/Italian textual messages are generated server-side by using the SimpleNLG realizer.

1 Introduction

Following a healthy diet plays a key role in the fulfillment of a good life. Artificial intelligence and ubiquitous computing are emerging technologies that can help people to eat in a correct way (e.g. (Mankoff et al., 2002; Kaptein et al., 2012; Hashemi and Javidnia, 2012)). Natural Language Generation (NLG) can be used in the diet context in different ways. NLG can be used to explain the results of numeric and symbolic reasoners (e.g. (Dragoni et al., 2017; Anselma et al., 2017)) or can be used to motivate users toward the best dietetic choice. Indeed, a number of projects have recently use NLG for guiding a user towards a virtuous behavior, among them (Reiter et al., 2003; Braun et al., 2018; Conde-Clemente et al., 2018).

MADiMan (Multimedia Application for Diet Management) is an ongoing project[1] with the aim to build a virtual assistant that is able to: recover the nutritional information directly from a specific recipe, reason over recipes and diets with flexibility, i.e. by allowing some forms of diet disobedience, and persuade the user to minimize such acts of disobedience (Anselma et al., 2017). The MADiMan architecture is composed by various

[1] http://di.unito.it/madiman

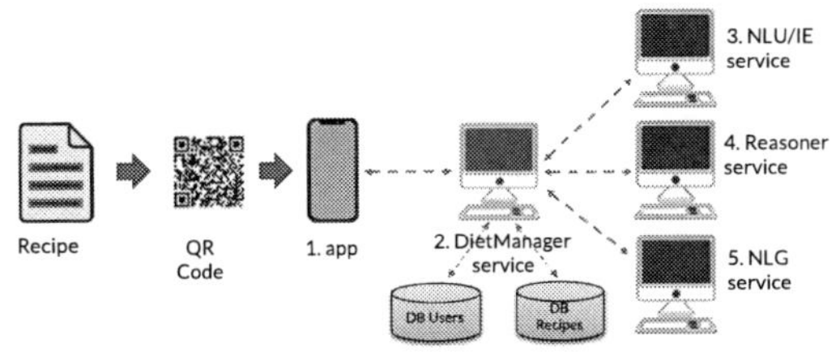

Figure 1: The MADiMan architecture.

modules (Fig. 1), that are a mobile app (described in Section 2), a numerical reasoner that decides the compatibility of a specific dish in some point of the diet (Anselma et al., 2017), an information extraction module used to compute the nutrient values of a specific recipe, a NLG service that converts the results of the computing to textual form (Anselma and Mazzei, 2017). The reasoning module of MADiMan overcame reasonable baselines in different simulation experiments (Anselma et al., 2017, 2018). We realized the CheckYourMeal! app in order to evaluate the performance and the usability of the whole architecture with human-evaluation into a realistic context. Moreover, we have recently used the app to test the appealing of the NL generated sentences in a first human-evaluation experiment (Anselma and Mazzei, 2018).

2 The CheckYourMeal! App and the NLG service

CheckYourMeal! is an iOS app[2] (developed in the Swift functional language) designed to present the result of the reasoning on food and diet in terms of both graphics and textual messages. The app is a prototype currently in a development stage.

In Fig. 2 we report three screenshots of the app.

[2] The app is currently in closed beta. Moreover, we plan to release an Android version in the next future.

Proceedings of the Workshop on Intelligent Interactive Systems and Language Generation (2IS&NLG), pages 45–47, Tilburg, The Netherlands, November 5 2018.

Figure 2: Three screenshots of CheckYourMeal.

The user interface is structured in three sections: the Home section, where the users are provided with general information, the Menu section, where the users can see the suggestions for the next meal and where they can input the chosen meals, and the Profile section, where the users can modify settings and user parameters. In the Menu section (central screenshot in Fig. 2), the user is presented with some suggestions of meals taken from a precompiled database of menus which are ordered by their distance from the ideal values of the dietary reference values. When a user selects a specific menu, CheckYourMeal! shows both (1) a pie-chart and (2) a textual message which contains information about the macronutrients values of the chosen menu.

The server (*DietManager service* in Fig. 1) is written in Java and it uses the Spring framework to communicate with the CheckYourMeal! app. The server calls the NLG service as an external Java library compacted into a single jar file. The NLG Service is composed by two submodules: (i) a monolithic rule-based document-sentence planner (Anselma and Mazzei, 2017) and, (ii) a bilingual English/Italian realizer defined over the SimpleNLG-it library (Mazzei et al., 2016). The entire NLG service has been developed by using the clojure language, that is a functional language running over the JVM.

The document and sentence planner follows simple fixed schemata. All messages will be composed by two parts: an overall evaluation of the dish and three evaluations for carbohydrates, lipids, proteins. The sentences generated for expressing the appropriateness of the specific macronutrients are positive copula sentences with a predicate expressing the deviation (i.e. rich/poor/perfect), and a PP modifier specifying the macronutrient (e.g. *in lipids*). Moreover, an adverb (e.g. *lightly*) distinguishes distinct deviations from the optimal choice. Note that the sentence plans generated are, apart from the lexicon, independent from the language used. So, the user selection of the language for the produced messages (English or Italian) corresponds to use a different realizer class of SimpleNLG-it. The actual implementation of the generator allows to select other two features concerning the lexicon (fixed or variable) and the aggregation strategy (VP and set aggregation). We have tested the app, by considering different values of the various features, in a first human-evaluation experiment with 20 people (Anselma and Mazzei, 2018).

During the demo session, we will show both the iOS app on a mobile phone and inner workings of the NLG Service.

3 Conclusion and Ongoing Work

In this paper we have presented the main features of CheckYourMeal!, an iOS app developed in the domain of the diet management. The app is used in the MADiMan architecture to provide the results of an automatic reasoner in terms of graphics and short text messages.

Future development concerns the implementation of a more sophisticated method for explanation in the text messages. We intend to integrate the numerical reasoning with ontological reasoning to obtain a causal explanation based over the past dishes. In the actual state of development the system allows for a limited form of human-machine interaction. In future work, we intend to experiment too a more sophisticated form of interaction based on dialogue, where the system could answer to questions concerning the compatibility of the menu in relation to the diet history.

References

Luca Anselma and Alessandro Mazzei. 2017. An approach for explaining reasoning on the diet domain. In *Proc. of the 1st Workshop on Natural Language for Artificial Intelligence co-located with AI*IA 2017, Bari, Italy.*. pages 4–17.

Luca Anselma and Alessandro Mazzei. 2018. Designing and testing the messages produced by a virtual dietitian. In *Proc. of 11th International Conference on Natural Language Generation (INLG 2018)*. ACL. To appear.

Luca Anselma, Alessandro Mazzei, and Franco De Michieli. 2017. An artificial intelligence framework for compensating transgressions and its application to diet management. *Journal of Biomedical Informatics* 68:58–70.

Luca Anselma, Alessandro Mazzei, and Andrea Pirone. 2018. Automatic reasoning evaluation in diet management based on an italian cookbook. In *Proceedings of the Joint Workshop on Multimedia for Cooking and Eating Activities and Multimedia Assisted Dietary Management*. ACM, New York, NY, USA, CEA/MADiMa '18, pages 59–62. https://doi.org/10.1145/3230519.3230595.

Daniel Braun, Ehud Reiter, and Advaith Siddharthan. 2018. Saferdrive: An nlg-based behaviour change support system for drivers. *Natural Language Engineering* 24(4):551–588. https://doi.org/10.1017/S1351324918000050.

Patricia Conde-Clemente, Jose M. Alonso, and Gracian Trivino. 2018. Toward automatic generation of linguistic advice for saving energy at home. *Soft Computing* 22(2):345–359. https://doi.org/10.1007/s00500-016-2430-5.

Mauro Dragoni, Tania Bailoni, Claudio Eccher, Marco Guerini, and Rosa Maimone. 2017. A semantic-enabled platform for supporting healthy lifestyles. In *Proceedings of the Symposium on Applied Computing*. ACM, New York, NY, USA, SAC '17, pages 315–322. https://doi.org/10.1145/3019612.3019835.

Baran Hashemi and Hossein Javidnia. 2012. Article: An approach for recommendations in self management of diabetes based on expert system. *International Journal of Computer Applications* 53(14):6–12. Published by Foundation of Computer Science, New York, USA.

Maurits Kaptein, Boris E. R. de Ruyter, Panos Markopoulos, and Emile H. L. Aarts. 2012. Adaptive persuasive systems: A study of tailored persuasive text messages to reduce snacking. *TiiS* 2(2):10.

Jennifer Mankoff, Gary Hsieh, Ho Chak Hung, Sharon Lee, and Elizabeth Nitao. 2002. Using low-cost sensing to support nutritional awareness. In *Proc. of the 4th int. conference on Ubiquitous Computing*. Springer-Verlag, London, UK, UbiComp '02, pages 371–376.

Alessandro Mazzei, Cristina Battaglino, and Cristina Bosco. 2016. SimpleNLG-IT: adapting SimpleNLG to Italian. In *Proceedings of the 9th International Natural Language Generation conference*. Association for Computational Linguistics, Edinburgh, UK, pages 184–192.

E. Reiter, R. Robertson, and L. Osman. 2003. Lessons from a Failure: Generating Tailored Smoking Cessation Letters. *Artificial Intelligence* 144:41–58.

Author Index

Association for Computational Linguistics
209 N. Eighth Street
Stroudsburg, Pennsylvania 18360

ISBN 978-1-5108-7756-6

CURRAN ASSOCIATES INC.
proceedings.com